What People Are Saying About

Making a Massacre

I am flabbergasted – I didn't know you had it in you! I'm trying to read through but I can't contain the laughter. This has to be the best thing I've ever read in my life. The great General Bilbo Baggins, the Father Ted references and my favourite: Mrs Cromwell washing the skidmarks out of Ollie's tighty whiteys. This is a profound and genius work of literary art. The mixture of biographical, historical and comedic content is fantastic and it keeps you gripped and entertained. I'm completely engrossed in it. Your defence of the truth and historical accuracy is heroic and it comes across very genuine in this piece. I've never been so excited for a book in my entire life.
The Outlaw MJ Podcast

Making a Massacre

Cromwell, Ireland and the
Slaughter of Innocents Scandal
(Not a Real History Book)

Making a Massacre

Cromwell, Ireland and the
Slaughter of Innocents Scandal
(Not a Real History Book)

Tomás Ó Raghallaigh

Winchester, UK
Washington, USA

CollectiveInk

First published by Liberalis Books, 2024
Liberalis Books is an imprint of Collective Ink Ltd.,
Unit 11, Shepperton House, 89 Shepperton Road, London, N1 3DF
office@collectiveinkbooks.com
www.collectiveinkbooks.com
www.liberalisbooks.com

For distributor details and how to order please visit the 'Ordering' section on our website.

Text copyright: Tomás Ó Raghallaigh 2023

ISBN: 978 1 80341 503 1
978 1 80341 542 0 (ebook)
Library of Congress Control Number: 2023935331

A CIP catalogue record for this book is available from the British Library.

Design: Lapiz Digital Services

Printed and bound by CPI Group (UK) Ltd, Croydon, CR0 4YY, UK

We operate a distinctive and ethical publishing philosophy in all areas of our business, from our global network of authors to production and worldwide distribution.

Contents

To Elowyn
What dreams may come

Acknowledgements

Keith Smith – fair play, man. Excellent title.

Paddy Goodwin – respect, you know what you did.

Oona Roycroft – seriously, thanks.

The Outlaw MJ – kudos, Marcus.

Noeleen, Cathy, Eóin and Myah – love yis!

Preface

Okay, enough is enough. I have already written four books that (when combined) completely exonerate Oliver Cromwell of massacring civilians on any significant scale in Ireland. (If you don't already know what he's accused of, you can't be Irish, you can't know anyone Irish, and you've probably never heard of Ireland.) According to Nielsen BookData, who know about these things, my books have not sold well in the overall scheme of things. Surprise, surprise. Clearly my conclusions are unpalatable to a typical Irish person when it comes to that bastard Cromwell. Or maybe they're just bad books.

Today, there are about 80 million people in the Irish diaspora worldwide who claim Irish ancestry. Even if only 70 million of them buy this book this would be deemed somewhat of a success. That villa in the South of France won't buy itself, you know!

In the publication *An Bullán* in 2001, Dr Jason McElligott wrote an article entitled 'Cromwell, Drogheda and the Abuse of Irish History' where he suggested that my work on Oliver Cromwell, up to that time, was abusing Irish history.

Well, Dr McElligott – you have your feckin' shite. I will see your opinions and raise you the actual truth of the matter. I would respectfully suggest that I'm not the one who is abusing Irish history. And this here book – as well as all of my other Cromwell books – proves this beyond all reasonable doubt.

Let's just have another quick example of this mistreatment of these historical events. In 2018 Irish schoolbook publisher CJ Fallon published a schoolbook called *History in Focus* that was written by Dan Sheedy. The offending words are as follows:

[Cromwell's] New Model army laid siege to Drogheda in September 1649. Following victory in the siege his forces entered the town and proceeded to massacre 3,500 civilians. Cromwell repeated this act during and after the Siege of Wexford in October that same year when a further 4,000 people were killed.

Christ on a bike! This is just not true. I literally can't even. And that's not an opinion – it's a fact! Don't you realise that Cromwell in Ireland has often been weaponised in the North of Ireland. Seriously, people?!

The message I have been peddling for years simply isn't getting through to the mainstream consciousness. Hence I offer to the world the story of my lifelong battle thus far to right a historical wrong and all the little bumps I encountered along the way. There are some who have accused me of committing some sort of treason against my country, Saorstát Eireann. To those lovely people I say – would yis ever grow up, for God sake! Besides, *táim effen an-bhródúil as a bheith Gaelach*. And while I'm at it – *an bfhuil cead agam dul amach le do thoil?*

Note to any would-be book reviewers out there: I've got a massive chip on my shoulder, I know – okay? My methods are unorthodox, I get that. Tear this book to shreds – I don't give a shite. But no matter what you do, you will never be able to dismiss my work outright. Facts is facts. And they cannot be argued with. The best have tried and failed. Namely, the famous five: Dr Jason McElligott, Prof. Micheál Ó Siochrú, Prof. Pádraig Lenihan, Prof. John Morrill and Timmy the dog whose attitude always stank. And speaking of Micheál Ó Siochrú, I've just decided to call myself Tomás Ó Raghallaigh for this particular publication because I suppose anyone with an Irish name can play at that game. I used to be called Tom Reilly but that was over five minutes ago now.

The humans above mentioned have published ardent (not to mention patronising) rebuttals of my work, examples of which feature very prominently here for all to see. It is these guys who provide me with the motivation to keep this (possibly doomed) crusade of mine going. You've only got yourselves to blame, guys. I haven't gone away, y'know.

Thing is – according to the facts – ye're all wrong. End of.

Cromwell was no genocidal maniac. This is my gift to the world. Now, get feckin' over it.

Chapter 1

1960–1993

Wanted – dead or alive

Now, children, if you're all sitting comfortably, I'll begin. I suppose the anonymous death threat is a good place to start. I think it was one of the lowest points. Or was it one of the highest? I can never decide. Anyway, I went all Salman Rushdie at the time. It was so odd. I had just turned 60 and I had been banging the 'Cromwell was really just an adorable misunderstood kitten' drum for about 20 years. The death threat was handwritten, and it had been dropped into the letterbox of my gaff. Wow. I must have done something really, really bad. I'm just one small step away from a fatwa here. How effen cool is that? Maybe there's a reward being offered. Imagine – a bounty on *my* head. Just how big a deal *is* this exactly?

Now, as it happens, I wasn't a big fan of death. Okay, it cuts down on expenses. That I get. But I had a plan for my life, and it didn't include death by death threat. When I die, I want it to be on my 100th birthday on the veranda of my beach house in Mauritius and I want my wife to be so upset that she drops out of university. In truth I was significantly more bemused than I was concerned. Incredibly, after a few taps on his phone, my son Eóin revealed the letter writer's identity. It took him less than five minutes. Wait, what?!

First question Eóin asked me was if there was anyone I had really, really pissed off.

'Seriously?!' I asked. 'Everybody Irish by now I would have thought.'

While that narrowed it down a bit, it didn't seem to be quite enough to identify an actual individual. He needed me to be more specific. How about lately? Who had I pissed off lately? Hmm. Now let me think. On Facebook maybe? Yes, of course! It's what I do: provocation on social media. A quick scan through my recent posts and boom! The language in the death-threat letter was practically the same as a particularly vitriolic comment from a clearly disgruntled Irish nationalist type. You know the sort: right-wing softcore republican, Catholic upbringing, completely unable to pronounce any words of the Irish National Anthem, a sometime pretend member of the RA, says he hates the gays but has a thing for Graham Norton that he doesn't fully understand. *Had* to be the same writer. Absolutely no question. The spelling mistakes matched. The contempt for me was the same. Shit, if that post got him mad, wait till he sees the swimsuit version of my book *Cromwell: An Honourable Enemy*. A Google search proved that our man had been a regular visitor to the local courthouse over the years. He wasn't quite a *complete* idiot. Some parts were clearly missing. But we got him. Well, that was easy.

It's a fair cop

Straight down to the cop station. Last time I was there I ended up in court myself for something I didn't do – I didn't run fast enough. See, as a teenager I used to suffer from kleptomania and when it got really bad I had to take something for it. Boys will be boys. But it was really nice to be on the other side of the fence this time – the victim. They take death threats very seriously there. Well, at least that's what the baffled cop at the desk said – at first.

'So, why would someone want to kill you?' he asked.

I found myself shifting from one foot to the other, trying hard to look like a potential murder victim. I really wanted to tell him that I had been heavily involved in the Kinahan/Hutch feud. Instead I found myself telling him that I had written some history books that some people didn't seem to like.

'They must be really bad,' he howled, finally unable to keep it in. In the end he said the guy was known to them and they thanked me for bringing it to their attention. I was just pleased I had provided them with some tea-break banter.

Drawda

Born, bred and buttered in Drogheda, the journey to death-threat status started when I became a young adult around 1992. Drogheda, or Drawda if you're a local, is located on the east coast of Ireland in the wee county of Louth, where we can thank geography and some sick joke between longitude and latitude for enduring a lifetime of horrendous weather along the River Boyne. Seriously – that east wind impales house pets and farmyard animals on sharp street furniture before it hits unsuspecting pedestrians on their daily constitutional. There are probably some things that you need to know about Drogheda before we move on. Well, there's *one* main thing really. It's the accent. We all know that there isn't really *one* Irish accent. Only five minutes down the road from anywhere in Ireland there's a different Irish accent. People from Dublin sometimes haven't a clue what other people from Dublin are talking about. A rugger bugger might say 'Isn't that roight, Finian?' Whereas a skanger might say, 'I will in me hoop, bud.'

However, not only is the Drawda accent unique, but everybody knows that Drawda people have their own language. It's a sort of incomprehensible sound that comes out of our mouths where we masafangle the English language in wurdz that only we understand. Expert linguists have labelled it the Maas Baa syndrome. Pardon me if I digress from the topic at hand momentarily.

It is a pacific affliction that renders locals incapable of saying the word flirt. And shirt is another tough one. A close relation is a cousint. Ulsters are bad but you can nearly die of ammonia. Hypochondriacts are always in the Lurdz Hostible, abuv in the Expensive Care Unit where they usually geh worser, or if you geh a throat infection you'd have to have your asteroids removed. Worser still, you could develop a brain tuba and have to geh an epidemic needle up your ass and God forbid, you could die and then vigour-mortis would set in.

But you're probly better off goin' to a fake healer. Or takin' Milk of Amnesia.

You can go on holidays to the Sea-shells, get starch naked. Write to the Omnibus Man, play the hobo, buy stuff at a jungle sale, and one of the greatest female jazz singers of all time was Elephants Gerald.

Drawda. Pure and simple.

Early tomfoolery

Sorry I went mad there for a second, as Father Ted would have said. So where was I? Oh yeah, the first 32 years of my life were pretty uneventful. Usual stuff. So lucky to have been born into the Catholic religion, the right religion. And everybody else is going to hell. Yeah, right. Took me a long time to finally exorcise religion from my body. But cast it out I eventually did. It's much more likely that we are the descendants of ancient bacteria than the children of God. DNA has created us, not the Almighty. How in God's own earth has religion gained such a foothold on God's own earth? Anyway, that's not a topic for here. That would be an ecumenical matter.

So, I had failed history at school back in 1978. Got an F in the Leaving Certificate. If you had told the Christian Brothers on Drogheda's Beamore Road, back then, that in a few short years I would completely rewrite one of the most controversial periods of Irish history, they would have pissed themselves. I was an errant teenager. I fought bitterly against authority, even if authority was oblivious to my adolescent hostility. But not long after I had kissed goodbye to my twenties, for some strange reason I found myself being drawn towards local history. Don't ask. I got nothing. No idea why. It's just one of those weird things that sometimes happen in life. I'm not exactly sure what part of the brain contains the local history cells, but whatever it is they began to animate me. By now I was married with two young kids, one of whom you've already met.

I had made little or no impact on my part of the wider world in Drawda and I was sailing along oblivious to most things that were happening elsewhere really. Still am, I suppose. Caught up in large doses of self-absorption, like most young folk. Usual ups and downs. You know how it is. On the bad days some mornings it even wasn't worth chewing through the leather straps. There were other days when I thought that my sole purpose in life was to be a lesson to others. Then on the good days I soared like a veritable eagle over the rich tapestry of mundane daily activities. And just when I discovered the meaning of life, they changed it.

Up the Mollies!

Because I live near the Mollies, a historically atmospheric part of the town of Drogheda, I became more specifically drawn to what happened there, hundreds of years ago. The crusade had begun. I think it was the blood-and-guts stuff that initially sparked my interest. The Mollies is where the breach was made in the wall when Cromwell came to town. A passionate advocate of all anti-Catholic laws, Cromwell was England's weapon of 'mass' destruction. I think it was the notorious terrorist Bilbo Baggins who once said that he didn't like battles because they were nasty, disturbing, uncomfortable things that made you late for dinner. Reckon he had a bit of an auld point there. Many of the Irish books I read seemed to reveal that this was a religious war, so basically killing each other over who's got the better imaginary friend then. I wasn't convinced that it was all about religion. There were lots of factors involved in this war, I would soon discover.

Many joined up to fight. Join the army, they said. Meet interesting people, they said. And then kill them. WTF? As one of the ballads of the day no doubt said at the time, this war, like the one before it and the one after it, was the war to end all wars. Probably even got to Number 1. Most men were made for war. So, many of them joined up to one side or the other. Of course it was an actual job – that they got real money for. Without it, they wandered about, getting under the feet of the women, who were trying to organise the really important things of life.

Heads literally rolled in this place as the battle for the town raged on 11 September 1649. Arms and legs were sliced open, cold hard metal plunged into torsos, as fathers, sons, uncles and even grandads were ripped to shreds in the appalling testosterone-fuelled orgy of death. Whatever way you look at it, it took some balls for those men to run straight into swords and pikes at a quarter past an idle Tuesday for a noble cause back in the day. Personally, I would never die for my beliefs because I might actually be wrong. It's no wonder the front line of the infantry was known as the 'forlorn hope'. Such was the savagery of the times, conscientious objectors were probably torn limb from limb and the remains boiled in their own blood by local rascal children. We really have no conception of what the barbarity of the times was like from this distance of years.

Accidentally becoming a historian

As my new-found thirst for knowledge inadvertently grew, I found myself advertently joining the Old Drogheda Society at the absurdly young age of 32. The majority of other members were at least twice my age. It was then that I began my search for articles and books about Cromwell at Drogheda. Oddly, there were none written by anybody local that I could find. While there were plenty of books on Cromwell himself, and thousands of others on the mid-seventeenth-century wars, I thought local was the way to go to find the perspectives I craved. Anyway, as all of the naffest writers say, it was then that I made the first decision that would change my life for ever – I made the short trip to the Drogheda Corporation offices and asked them if they had any records that dated from 1649, the year of the siege. They had. Mad Ted.

Des Foley, the Drogheda Town Clerk at the time, very kindly gave me access to the strong room in his office. After a few minutes of small talk that neither of us really wanted to pursue, he left me alone with an ancient book. It was entitled *The Council Book of the Corporation of Drogheda*. More significantly, it dated from 1649, the very year I hoped would be included. What a happy coincidence! A complete novice at understanding the context of historical documents, it was some time before I realised that it wasn't a coincidence at all. The previous records had been either lost or destroyed in the storming of the town that year. Well, duh.

The book itself was absolutely mesmerising to me: the earthy fragrance of the musty cover, the woody scent of the thick vellum pages, the eloquence of the stunning ink handwriting all immediately transported me right back to the time when it was written. This was the actual book that the town recorder wrote the town's activities into in the days following Cromwell's siege of Drogheda! I could imagine the stuffy old town official sitting somewhere in a building close by that is now long gone in a medieval townscape, the aesthetics of which I could barely grasp with my modern eyes. The feckin' recorder probably even met Cromwell. The feeling that I experienced of actually touching the history in this book was completely absorbing. It was like nothing I had ever felt before. Somehow, it was like all of the intervening centuries had not happened at all. I had gone straight back to the time itself. I was in. It was quite a profound moment.

So, I got down to work. I had been taught at school that the vast majority of the citizens of the town were slaughtered by

Cromwell. Three thousand people in all. It was a thing. Part of your DNA, if you're from Drogheda. You hate that murdering English bastard because he came over here and killed all of Drogheda's citizens. My ancestors. Well, on a wider scale of course everybody Irish hates him, I suppose, but since Drogheda was the biggest stain on his career, we have a special dose of animosity in our hearts for the fecker. And I felt it to my bones. This inherent bitterness towards him among Droghedeans has fermented over the centuries. And as a chisler growing up around here, I drank bottles of the stuff.

Out of Ireland have we come. Great hatred, little room,
Maimed us at the start. I carry from my mother's womb
A fanatic heart. W.B. Yeats

To somebody from Drogheda, saying the word Cromwell is the same as saying the word Hitler to a Jew, Pol Pot to a Cambodian, Alex Ferguson to a Liverpool fan. The same images of malevolence are conjured up. It's inevitable. There's really nothing you can do about it. We don't fight it. We embrace it. We are inspired by it. And we hate the English because of it. Of all the 800 years of oppression, 1649 was definitely one of the worst. So, here was an actual contemporary record. In my very own hands. I couldn't wait to read all about the details of the siege from actual eyewitnesses and to see what the townspeople thought of Cromwell.

Then came the first surprise – there wasn't even a mention of the siege in the Corporation records. The entire population wiped out? And nothing? Are you for serious? The biggest event that had ever happened to the town and those that lived here at that time seem to have completely missed it. What?! Holy mother of divine… Well, except to say that the September Corporation meeting was postponed because of the 'then troubles'. What on earth was going on? I was stunned! Even more strangely, there were hundreds of names of local people documented who simply went about their daily business in the days, weeks and months after the siege. Now, hang on a second. Should all these people not be dead? Their shredded flesh and smashed bones scattered to the four corners of the town? Am I missing something?

Apart from bad essays at school, I had never really written anything before. I definitely wasn't one of those literary types who wanted to write the great Irish novel. I didn't even want to read the great Irish novel. But c'mon. This was crying out to be written. Locally, no local had ever written in a local way about the local historical event of the millennium to have happened locally. But I'm a local. So why not me? I figured I could throw a few words on a page that might, at a stretch, seem coherent. Okay, this was history. What the feck did I know about history?! When I did the Leaving Cert, I had no idea what the difference was between the Black 'n Tans and the Fenians. They were all just noises that came out of my history teacher John Garvey's mouth. Most of his words got in the way of my teenage carnal musings during history class; not mentioning any names, Gillian Murphy, Deirdre Kelly and Margaret Sharkey. Pearl Harbor? Who is she? Did Magna Carta die in vain? They all laughed at Joan of Arc, but she went right ahead and built it. See – not a clue. And yet as the newest member of the ODS I had the temerity to ask the then chairman Seán Collins if I should write an article on Cromwell at Drogheda. He told me to go for it. Although I wasn't convinced that he was convinced.

A reading from the first book of Reilly

In September 1993 my first book *Cromwell at Drogheda* was printed. Not published. Printed. The article I had started soon grew into a book. Being a director of printing company Broin Print Ltd at that time came in particularly handy. Without exerting too much pressure on my minions, I had 1,000 copies printed and effectively it only cost the company the price of the paper, printing plates and ink. I knew nothing about the publishing world, but I had worked in the printing industry since I was a teenager. It was a typically basic self-published book that just outlined the facts really. It wasn't in the least bit controversial. Seán suggested that I donate the proceeds to the society, which I was happy to do. This was mainly because they could sell them, and I didn't have to. And since it had cost me nothing, what did I have to lose?

It wasn't controversial of course because I had absolutely no notions about myself whatsoever at that time. The notions – about challenging the verdict of history – would come later. Sure, in this research I discovered things that seemed to contradict what I was taught at school – but who the feck was I to question the world? Nobody, that's who. Generations of academics had studied this period and the conclusion was resounding: Cromwell was a murdering git, and don't anyone ever question it. Besides, my research mainly consisted of attending the local library and cobbling together a chronological sequence of events related to the storming of the town, highlighting all things local along the way. The boffins beyant in Oxbridge were unlikely to be quaking in their boots any time soon.

The best thing about that first book was the book launch. I loved it. Such a buzz. Here I was, like a bride on her wedding day, a famous footballer in a pub, an altar boy at a priests' convention – the complete centre of attention. Everybody wanted a piece of me. Signing books became a thing. Wow! People were actually queueing up for my autograph. What gives. Then in the coming weeks and months the book went on to have a life of its own. I'd meet people in the street and, as an author now, I would purposely assume an erudite air. I didn't realise I was just being a dick and I was perfectly happy talking down to non-author types who, in my eyes, seemed to respect my new-found sophistication. Come and appreciate me now, people, and avoid the rush. This book thing. How buzzy was this? I was hooked. People used to come up to me and say, 'Tom, do people really come up to you?' I got to the stage where when I used to bore people I could tell that they thought it was their fault.

Widening my horizons

The wider subject of Cromwell in Ireland completely began to fascinate me. I couldn't get enough of it. On a family trip to Galway, in the famous Kenny's Bookshop, I discovered a first edition of Father Denis Murphy's *Cromwell in Ireland* that was published in the nineteenth century. The bould Murph excoriated Cromwell from a height. Civilians had been massacred by the bucketload wherever Cromwell went in Ireland. He nailed Irish babies to church doors while he was waiting for his eggs to boil for his breakfast. But after what I was starting to find out about Drogheda and Cromwell, the cynic in me wasn't quite convinced that every word the good priest wrote was necessarily true.

I learned that, after Drogheda, Wexford was also badly hit by those bastard roundheads. I remember thinking: imagine if I researched Wexford and I discovered that loads of civilians were still alive after Cromwell's visit there too? How come nobody is seeing this? Immersing myself in the topic, I started to pick up Cromwelly books everywhere. It was only when I picked up Wilbur Cortez Abbott's *The Writings and Speeches of Oliver Cromwell* that I found a nugget of primary source evidence that completely intrigued me. Following the horrific massacres of Drogheda and Wexford, Ollie wrote the following words: 'Good now, your words are massacre, destroy and banish. Give us an instance since my coming into Ireland of one man, not in arms, massacred, destroyed or banished.' WTAF? Not only was this guy a murdering bastard but he was also a lying git! How could he possibly say that? After Drogheda *and* Wexford?

I never really planned a research strategy. It was more a case of just keep reading about the subject. I never wrote any notes or anything. As it seeped slowly into my psyche, I gradually felt compelled to travel to the places that were associated with Ollie. In Ireland, these places were primarily Wexford and Clonmel. I threw Kilkenny in for good measure. But what held the most fascination for me were the places in England where he himself lived and frequented. They were: Huntingdon, where he was born and lived during his early years; Cambridge, where he went to college; St Ives, where he rented a property during a particularly challenging time in his life; and Ely, in a house he inherited and where he lived when he came to prominence in the English Civil Wars.

Cromwell the utter, utter bastard. Case closed

I also discovered that four years after he battered the shite out of Ireland, Ollie actually became the Lord Protector of England, Scotland and Ireland. So, this guy was an unqualified tyrant and it seems nothing was going to stand in his way to get to the very top as a power-hungry monster. It's no wonder that everybody hates him. Even the English, according to reports I had read, since they dug up his body after his death and hung it on the gallows at Tyburn before drawing and quartering it for the baying crowd. Okay, there may be small anomalies in the records that as yet made no real sense to me. But clearly Cromwell was a Catholic-hating, -butchering military dictator who slaughtered thousands of ordinary Irish people on his uncompromising crusade to ultimate power. Brace yourself for more cheese – I wasn't to know it at the time, but I couldn't have been more wrong. About everything. End chapter.

Chapter 2

1993–1999

Ollie! Ollie! Ollie! Oi! Oi! Oi!

Standing in the kitchen of Oliver Cromwell's actual house in Ely completely blew my mind. It was three years since the book came out and I was just digging deeper into this subject with every passing month. Not only does his house still exist today, but it's actually a tourist attraction nowadays. And it's called Oliver Cromwell's House. Go figure. Here I was looking at the very sink in which old Mrs Cromwell probably washed the skidmarks off her husband's ye olde tightie whities. I stood in front of the same hearth where the man himself must have stood warming his arse before embarking on a hard day's work of raping, pillaging and slaughtering. It was quite a moving experience. I had been to Wexford and Clonmel by this time and I had gotten a full understanding of all his dastardly deeds there. But I needed to make the trip to Cambridgeshire – Cromwell country – to fully understand the man. Now here I was. Immersing myself in *terribly* English versions of Cromwell for the very first time.

While he was born in Huntingdon, nearby Ely was the highlight for me because of this house. It lies just yards from the gargantuan edifice of Ely Cathedral. Every room I went into were rooms in which the old warty git himself had a myriad of experiences and feelings. Both the geography and topography of the house were exactly as he would have experienced it. These were the banisters that he would have slid down after a few bevvies. This was the oak-panelled closet where he must have spanked the bejaysus out of the Cromwellian monkey when he was stressed. It was through this back door that he would have bolted to get to the outside loo when he got the skitters after a night on the lash. In this very bedroom his two daughters Mary and Frances were conceived. Trying to imagine the actual positions of conception was probably a step too far, but I went there anyway. Word to the wise – Oliver Cromwell having sex is not really a place you want to go to.

Here was the drawing room where the Cromwells would have put up their Christmas tree and where Santa would have left the presents. Now, hang on just a second. Did Cromwell himself not actually ban Christmas? This is one of the things that he's famous for throughout the world, is it not? Turns out that was just a load of auld shite as well. *No*, is clearly and absolutely the answer.

At this early stage of the story he's still a complete and absolute thundering bollix. And that was exactly the page that I was still on. It would take some time yet for my views to change. It was while he was living in this very house that OC rose to some prominence in the outside world. It was here that he first joined the parliamentarian army after parliament had fallen out with King Charles I. It was from this house that he went from being a gentleman farmer to the most successful English commander of the English Civil War.

Cromwell the nipper

Today Huntingdon, the town in which he was reared, is a less pretty town than Ely, with fewer chocolate-box houses for the delectation of the blue-rinse culture vulture brigade. As a result it's harder to imagine what it was like in the seventeenth century. But the school where OC attended as a nipper still exists today. The building on the High Street houses the Cromwell Museum. I wouldn't get too excited. It could also pass for the smallest museum in England if it weren't for the Warley Museum that is housed in a West Yorkshire telephone box and is officially the smallest museum in England. I strolled around the one-roomed building trying to take it all in. This is where the psychotic beast did his ABCs, his times table, his history, geography and most significantly his religion classes. This is where he must once have daydreamed, like all kids do, of future disembowellings, decapitations, hangings and murders. Aw, bless. There was a wax mannequin of him as a kid; a black hat he used to actually wear as an adult; one of his swords; paintings, busts, coins: there was Cromwell stuff everywhere. Well, it *was* the Cromwell Museum.

But to one with an Irish sensibility there was something odd about these two places: his house and his school. Something that I genuinely hadn't counted on. This *was* Oliver Cromwell, right? The English Adolf Hitler? The man who killed civilians for fun? The man to whom any good Catholic was a dead Catholic. But in the portrayal of the man in both of these visitor attractions there wasn't a mention of his wholesale massacres in Ireland. Not a one. What the...? Could this get any weirder? These people were glorifying him as some sort of historical enigma; a family man who rose to great heights from abject mediocrity; the slayer of a tyrannical king, perhaps even the first republican; the father of English democracy, a noble warrior, the founder of the English army itself – all of which he did by complete accident and, you could be forgiven for thinking, with one hand tied behind his back.

Now, who is this person exactly?

I had fully expected my visit to Wexford earlier in the year to quash the suspicions I had nurtured about Drogheda when it came to the wholesale deaths of unarmed local yokels at OC's hands there. Surely here there could be absolutely no doubt that Wexfordian babies, toddlers, uncles, aunts, grannies, grandads were slaughtered indiscriminately. It's in the history books, FFS. But while there was plenty of tradition and folklore of horror stories embedded into his legacy in the sunny south-east, hard evidence of actual civilian atrocities was just as difficult to nail down as it had been in Drogheda. And now here I was in England and it was like they were talking about a totally different person altogether. Now I was really confused. So there was really only one thing for it – I simply *had* to wipe the slate clean. I had to get rid of the prejudices that were ingrained in me from childhood. I had to recalibrate my brain and emerge as a person who had no Cromwell baggage whatsoever. From this point onwards, that was going to be my default position.

Furthermore, I decided that I would home in on primary source evidence, whatever the hell that was. I had begun to realise that accounts of the period were less and less accurate, and more and more partisan, the further away in time from the events they were written. Cromwell was the most written-about English head of state ever. And because he was such a complex figure, most writers had an axe to grind, either *for* or *against* him. Irish writers castigated him from a height at every turn. Well, they would, wouldn't they? English writers, not so much. The figure is now approaching about 4,000 published books on the man. Was it possible that all those things that I was taught about OC at school were all wrong? Oh dear, I think I can feel another book coming on.

'An honourable enemy' is conceived

While in the UK, I was exposed to a lot of books that I hadn't seen or heard of previously. In a Cambridge bookshop I picked up a few gems. Roger Howell's *Images of Oliver Cromwell* accidentally became the catalyst for my next project. It was a collection of essays by different academics, and I was quickly drawn to an essay by the famous historian and Cromwell expert Toby Barnard entitled 'Irish Images of Oliver Cromwell'. In his paper Barnard proposed the idea that OC was actually 'an honourable enemy'. The old me would have thought the whole notion of that murdering bastard being honourable was completely shocking and bordering on hilarious. But the new me with my burgeoning notions of his possible innocence in areas yet to be determined thought: what a wonderful title for a book – *Cromwell: An Honourable Enemy*. That will really piss some people off. Imagine if that actually turns out to be the case. Sheesh.

Developing notions, or as I like to call it – book two

When I returned from my UK Cromwell odyssey, I got right down to it. Let's write this feckin' book. Having visited the main Cromwell locations both in Ireland and across the water, and picked up books and articles in each one, I was ready to put pen to paper, well, fingers to keyboard. In the traditional massacre story, certain red flags had now presented themselves to me. In Abbott's *Writings and Speeches of Oliver Cromwell*, OC's orders to his troops when he arrived at Dublin on 15 August were quite clear: 'I do hereby warn every soldier or officer under my command, not to do any wrong or violence to any persons whatsoever, unless they be in arms or office with the enemy, as they shall answer to the contrary at their utmost peril.' Then there was his statement where he categorically denied killing 'one man, not in arms', after Drogheda and Wexford. And what about the whole idea of all those Drogheda people milling around the town after the siege as if they were normal when they were clearly supposed to be dead? So there were no eyewitness details of civilian deaths at Wexford. Nor were there any at Drogheda. All is not what it seems. The thick plottens.

I began to write. During this bit I became more and more convinced that OC was indeed an honourable enemy, as we will see. It was really the only thing that fitted the facts that I was now uncovering with my clean slate. So I went for it. While this was clearly a means to an end, as I just wanted to get the word out, I also began to enjoy the entire writing process. Throwing words up in the air and seeing where they landed. That sort of stuff. During my research I became aware of the work of local amateur historians Harold O'Sullivan and Father Gerry Rice, who were also sceptical about the wholesale civilian massacre stories. Hmm, so I wasn't the only one then. I like it. That gave me even more confidence.

Nine months later and sometime during early 1998, I had written all I had to write about the matter. It was about 80,000 words. It just kinda spewed out of me. In the back of my mind I had completely ruled out citations simply because I hadn't a clue what they were all about. Not a notion. I was completely oblivious to the fact that I was creating a historical work. To me it was simply text. Historians could worry about their endnotes and footnotes and how they should be meticulously presented with perfect punctuation and clarity. But a Jack-the-lad like me who had failed history – you have your shite. No point in even trying. I wasn't going to pretend that I was some sort of historian when I clearly wasn't.

Naturally, having looked around at all the books that were out there about OC, I did feel that my take on this controversial topic was quite different. I was telling a radical story about the events. And this needs a wider audience. And so I decided to investigate the idea of getting an actual book publisher. Someone who would invest in my work and who had the necessary distribution systems to reach much further than I ever could if I simply had it printed by a local printer. Yet the risk to this particular prospect was huge. Because as soon as an adult in the history business would read it, I was bound to be exposed as a charlatan – a gobshite who was just chancing his arm.

Trying to get published

In the late 1990s, of course, the word Google had not quite become a verb in this neck of the woods yet, but I was all over it even as a noun. I discovered oodles of publishers on the World Wide Web. Finding a publisher should be a piece of piss, I thought to myself. They'll be falling over themselves when they see what I have to say. Boy, was I wrong. Following their respective strict submission guidelines, I began to send e-mails to the publishers of non-fiction books. It seemed that I got significantly more rejection letters than the number of publishers I had originally contacted. Twenty-five. Forty. Fifty. Every one of them a rejection. But out of a mixture of both sheer thickness and misplaced confidence, I kept going. I was that sad I actually kept count of the number I had contacted and after 70 fruitless book pitches I was getting quite despondent. Damn. I was sure I had discovered a fundamental flaw in the teaching of Irish history. How are people not getting this?

Good news sprinkled with bad news

Like in all the best happy ending dramas, one day at work the bat phone rang. It was Steve McDonagh from Brandon Books in Dingle.

'Good news, Tom,' he said, or words to that effect. 'We would like to publish your book.'

There are fewer buzzes in the world that are as buzzy as this particular expression. I clearly remember asking him how many the print run would be. Then came the hold-your-horses moment: 'Can you send me the version with references?'

My heart sank. Apparently, in the history business you have to be able to quote your sources. Otherwise you could say anything. I didn't bullshit the man. I told him there were none. I was beginning to lose him, so I had to think fast. In that instant I wondered: well, how hard can it be? If kids at school can do this, what's my problem? I told him that if he gave me a month, I'd stick them in. Endnotes. Footnotes. Blue notes. Sticky notes, high notes, low notes. Whatever he wanted. Fair play to Steve. Instead of running for cover he agreed to wait for the endnotes.

The best way to describe the next three months (it took that long) is a memory test. Now, where the hell did I read that? And what about that? Where did I see that? As far as I was concerned all I had to do was to quote the actual publication in which I had found the reference. The difference between primary and secondary sources was *never* on my radar. This was a nightmare. I had never stood in a third-level institution where this stuff was taught. Where they ate, drank and slept endnotes, footnotes and whatever-you're-having-yourself notes. I didn't know what kind of statements or quotations even needed to be referenced. Them all? Some of them? Which ones? So I just guessed and hoped for the best.

The carrot was a published book in the grown-up book world. So I kept going. To say that I erred on the side of caution with the endnotes is probably an understatement. With the addition of the references, the document ended up at 140,000 words. But in all fairness it was in much better shape. The relief when Steve finally accepted my finished manuscript without question was humongous. It was August 1998 and I was delighted to know that in a couple of weeks I'd have the book in my hands. This time, it would be published.

'So what we talking here, Steve? Two/three weeks?' Having been in the printing business for years, I know how these things work. So, don't bullshit me now, Steve.

'May, next year,' said the bould Steve, probably without batting an eyelid. I couldn't tell. He was on the phone in Dingle.

Ten months?! Yup. That's the publishing process. For books like mine, it takes the guts of a year to publish. Well, all good things lie in anticipation as that bloke Job outta that famous novel, the Bible, once famously said; so I just completely swallowed any idealistic protestations I had and hoped I'd still be around in ten months' time, which was a lifetime away.

Somewhere in between all of this I began to encounter real historians. This was mainly due to the fact that I would shoot my mouth off at any given opportunity and I invariably got their attention. In the early days I fully expected erudite push-backs from those whose actual business this was, and into which I had just stumbled. But that just didn't happen. And the more I wasn't challenged about my thesis, the more I just pushed my luck.

Enter Historian A

During this time I went to a history lecture by an up-and-coming academic. From the moment this young buck started to open his mouth I was completely enthralled. I wanted to have this guy's children. He was energetic, distinctive, effusive and he flung words at his audience like they were stuck in his throat, barely stopping to take a breath. Not like the stuffy academic stereotypes in tweed with leather-patch elbows I had imagined at all! The phrase that came to mind was 'history at pace'. I was excited. Buoyed up. I couldn't wait for the Q&A at the end.

When the dynamic rollercoaster of information had ended, I got a chance to ask this cool bastard a question. This is gonna be brilliant. He's bound to engage me in conversation here in the lecture hall and our discourse will blow the heads off the entire audience, bar none. Then we'd probably go to a pub later on when his jaw would hit the floor when I would tell him the stuff I've discovered. He would be completely bound to say something like the following: 'Oh my God, Tom, how did you find all that out? All on your own? And you an amateur? This is huge! This changes our whole understanding of the entire period as we know it. I personally thank you. History thanks you. Posterity thanks you.' And I would say something back like: 'I know, right?' He'd look at me. I'd look at him. We'd smile. Our loins would stir. The chemistry would be undeniable. Then we would probably kiss. If he didn't make the first move, I was definitely gonna. Worst-case scenario – we'd be BFFs for life.

So one might imagine my surprise when Historian A looked at me like I had two heads after my question assailed his ears. I had asked him if he had been aware of the work of Harold O'Sullivan and Father Gerry Rice concerning the accuracy

25

of the civilian massacre stories. To describe his reaction as contemptuous is pretty accurate. I can still see his face glaring at me with disdain as he proceeded to outline the reasons why Ollie killed civilians at Drogheda and why on earth would anyone want to question that? The other feeling I got was that he wanted me to know that he was the historian in the room and that he knew his shit. I had no argument whatsoever with that! And yet, I was dying to tell him that I had written a book on the subject that challenged his opinion, but I was petrified in case I'd be the laughing-stock of the room. So I passed.

A book publicist? Pour little old *moi*? Surely you jest

Back in my fantasy world, to say that I hounded Steve, Siobhán and Máire in Brandon over the next nine months or so is probably an exaggeration. But it was something very akin to hounding. I followed the publication process like a dog with a bone. On the day I corrected my first proof sheets I was as proud as a schoolboy who had just gotten his first dose of the clap. I was so tuned to the production schedule when it *finally* came around that I drove to Future Print in Baldoyle to get the first book hot off the presses. There is simply nothing better than that feeling of holding your own book in your own hand. It was a hardback. I was literally beside myself with excitement. And what's more, Steve had organised a book publicist for me, which meant that I was obviously an extremely important individual at that time. With a significant story to tell. Feck Historian A. He had melted back into the academic bubble from which he had emerged and I was unlikely to ever encounter him again. Yeah, right.

The thing about the book was that not only was it reviewable, it was also somewhat newsworthy. On 30 April in the *Cambridge Evening News*, reporter Ann Patey published an article entitled 'Irishman claims that Cromwell was Framed'. Hmm, I liked that phrase. On 2 May John Burns wrote a news piece in the *Sunday Times* – 'Cromwell's Irish campaign was beyond reproach, says historian'. Okay, so now this is getting ridiculous. Why on earth would anyone call me a historian? At every given opportunity I tried to tell people that I failed history at school. Now the *Sunday Times* is calling me a historian. But I was completely getting off on the fact that I *wasn't* a historian. Grrr. This was the point! On 7 May the *Irish Mirror* ran a piece where they interviewed Belfast cleric Monsignor Denis Faul. The headline read: 'Cromwell was fiend says Irish priest. He slams book praising "hero"'. I'm very annoyed with this book,' said Mgr Faul. 'It gives the impression that Cromwell was a nice man when he was more like Milosevic or even Hitler.'

Oh shit

Soon an interview schedule came through from my publicist Linda Kenny – by fax. Aw, bless. Remember faxes? There were also interviews scheduled for local radio stations by the score, the *Pat Kenny Show* on RTE Radio 1 being the highlight. Notification that the book was to be reviewed in various periodicals followed, the first one of which to appear on the streets would be the *Irish Times*! My family, parents, my uncles, aunties, cousins and even my casual acquaintances were incredibly proud that this council estate nut job was about to turn Irish history on its head. Brace yourself, Ireland. Here I come, world. This is gonna be awesome. I quickly embraced the fact that I was about to lose my obscurity. Next stop, *This Is Your Life*!

This was really the day of publication for me. This would be the very first time that I would see what real actual people thought of my spectacular revelations. Saturday 8 May 1999 dawned. My wife Noeleen and I went to have breakfast in Monks' café on Drogheda's North Quay. After a few minutes I built up the courage to nip around the corner into Madame Le Worthy's in Shop Street to buy the *Irish Times*. Surely in just a few weeks I would be given an honorary degree by Trinity College after they read this. The headline read 'Cleaning Up

Cromwell'. Ooooh, so far so good. I like it! It was written by a Professor Kevin Whelan who was Michael Smurfit Director of the Keough-Notre Dame Centre in Dublin. Nope. Never heard of it. It's far from Keough-Notre Dame Centres I was reared.

The newspaper was actually shaking in my hands as I digested the good professor's review. I had to start over a few times because I just could not concentrate with the exhilaration racing through my body. Get ready, Ireland – here I come! I'm about to develop a reputation that I'll have a lot of trouble living up to!

'None of this is convincing,' he wrote. 'There is an interesting book to be written about Cromwell in Ireland; this is not it,' was Kevin Whelan my brand-new adversary's parting salvo. The anticipation in the pit of my stomach transformed into acidic bile in seconds. How I didn't projectile vomit over all the half-awake breakfast clientele in Monks' is beyond me.

'*None* of this is convincing.' What, like *none*? Not *one* word? You for serious? Oh my God, I've been found out already, and it's only day one.

Chapter 3

1999

This is not good. Steve – a little help?

If I was being *completely* honest, I would probably have *kinda* agreed with Kevin Whelan's assessment of the book myself. As a complete chancer, I had expected a lot of push-back. And here it was already in full living colour. I was still trying to figure out how in God's name I was the only one saying this about Cromwell in this day and age. So, despite how Mr Whelan made me feel, he was probably right. Jaysus. What have I done? That didn't last long. Aw, sure, I'll have a bit of craic with it and see what mileage I can get out of the book at least.

In no world was this right. An F in Leaving Cert history? Changing our perception of seismic historical events? Seriously? What *was* I thinking? It's completely ridiculous of course. Could never happen. It's simply not plausible. Worst-case scenario: so far I seem to have hoodwinked a publisher, and some peer reviewers, maybe. No real damage done. I'll shut up now and get back into my box. Okay, so Mr Whelan had assailed my ego. I wanted everybody to love me and think I was great. The *Irish Times* had spoken. And where I come from, that's a big thing. Well, the *Drogheda Independent* is bigger there, but that's just splitting hairs on a rolling stone that's gathering no moss. Cromwell was a civilian-murdering bollix. Sure, everybody knows that.

But then again, in his review, Kevin Whelan didn't exactly dismantle my arguments with erudite counter-arguments that I simply could not ignore. Actually, come to think of it, he didn't offer any arguments at all. He just simply said that it wasn't convincing.

Steve was incensed. Well, maybe not quite incensed, but he was certainly miffed enough to write a letter to the *Irish Times* complaining about the review. 'Had your reviewer actually reviewed the book and found fault with its thesis,' wrote Steve, 'one could have no complaint. But for most of the review he paraded his own ideas about Cromwell; he scarcely acknowledged the book or its thesis but merely dismissed them.' But Steve didn't leave it there. 'There is an interesting review to be written about *Cromwell: An Honourable Enemy*; this was not it,' was his parting salvo. Genius, I thought to myself. That's just so clever. I took some solace from the fact that it must have been very rare for a publisher to write to a newspaper following a review of one of their books. It's just not the done thing. Go me.

Aw, Gawd

The *Sunday Tribune* carried a review on the day after Whelan's appeared, and it was written by Pauric Travers, head of the History Department at St Patrick's College, Drumcondra. The subheading read: 'Pauric Travers is unconvinced by a reinterpretation of Oliver Cromwell's Irish campaign'. Okay, this is not going well. This guy was the rale McCoy. An actual historian. Probably had the leather patches on his elbows and everything. I'm fecked. My burgeoning reputation is fast being flushed down the toilet.

At this point I remember coming to terms with the fact that I just needed to try and come away from this embarrassing episode with some pride left intact. I've clearly humiliated myself in front of the whole of the Old Drogheda Society, my family and friends and the people who helped me with the research for the book with my delusions of grandeur. It's a fair cop, governor.

Hang on! Hang on!

I had to wait a week for the next review, and it came in the guise of the *Irish Independent*. Charles Chenevix Trench was the reviewer. 'A New Model of Cromwell', was the hilarious headline pun. (For the uninformed, the New Model Army was associated with Cromwell. Oliver's army and all that. Jeez, do I have to explain *everything*?) After Whelan's piece, I really had to brace myself for this one. 'Tom Reilly has done a terrific job of research to make a case for Cromwell against the verdict of history...this is a very praiseworthy effort. We hope for more from Tom Reilly.'

Wait, what?

Well, shiver me timbers, hold the front page, fetch me a feather boa and call me Tomasina! I couldn't believe it! Wow. Somebody actually gets it. Maybe this isn't such a disaster after all. Linda had told me about all the reviews that were coming up and, as the rollercoaster had already taken off, I had no choice now but to just hang on for dear life. But fair play to Charles Chenevix Trench! After all that research, some of it had to stick. I knew it. I just knew it. I must have made some good points. *Some* of them must have been convincing. I'm not a complete idiot.

Hmm...

The following day in the *Sunday Business Post*, in her review, Mary Cullen wrote: 'If Reilly is right and he appears to make a strong case...if he succeeds in de-demonising our collective image of the man, he could help us to focus instead on the long-term political developments in which Cromwell was a leading player.' A strong case, eh? Okay, it's not bad. It doesn't really say I'm brilliant. But I'll let Mary off. She seems like a decent type. Maybe she read the convincing parts and still needed some convincing. But hang on a second, folks; then came the big one.

Good holy lantern Jaysus!

Things were about to get interesting. Very interesting indeed.

The following week, I was sitting at home and I get a call from my English cousin Ian who lives in London.

'Well, looks like you hit the big time, cuz,' he said. I had no idea what he meant. 'I've just bought the *Sunday Times* and the front cover of the book supplement is a review of your book.'

'Well, holy God,' as Miley would have said. 'Is it a good one or a bad one?' I asked him nervously.

'Buy it and see, you cheap bastard,' came the reply.

The English version of the *Sunday Times*! It was by Ruth Dudley Edwards. 'The Good Soldier' was the headline. While modesty prevents me from repeating the entire review here in full, here are just a few snippets. After outlining the traditional version of Cromwell that we all know and love so much, the bould RDE wrote:

> But now comes this book by Tom Reilly, a Drogheda amateur historian (and the owner of a software recycling company for heaven's sake), which humbles us all. Reilly's elaborate documentation and careful analysis destroys the distortions and inventions produced later to suit the agendas first of royalists then of nationalists. The evidence of contemporary writers is that there was no murder of civilians in Drogheda, Wexford or anywhere else...Although professional historians are prone to be sniffy about amateurs, I have always believed they should be given a special accolade for being in love with their subject for its own sake...he is scrupulous in his examination of evidence, he has the necessary scepticism, he is assiduous in research and he quotes primary sources extensively. Above all he understands that the past should not be judged by the standards and fashions of the 1990s. Would that we could say that of the majority of those who these days teach history for a living.

It goes without saying that now I wanted to have Ruth Dudley Edwards' babies. Straight in, no kissing. There and then. I had no idea who she was, but she was now my bestest friend in the whole wide world. Kevin Whelan's opinions were easily cast to the mists of time. I could now die happy. This was the *Sunday Times* FFS. And I was on the front cover of the book supplement that week! Does it get any better than this? Oh, and ignore the 'owner of a software recycling company' bit – that's the real world and it has absolutely no place in this tale. Back in my Cromwell journey, I was now on cloud nine. Whatever happened in the rest of my life, the *Sunday Times* (both English and Irish versions) meant that I could now hold my head up high and take the blows wherever they were going to land. Some of this *was* indeed convincing. I feckin' knew it!

Trouble at t' mill

It was around then that I was asked to talk at a symposium/ conference/seminar/convention on historical things somewhere in a location in Europe that I can never mention to protect the protagonists' identities. When I was told that Historian A was also doing a talk too, well, you can imagine my excitement. This is brilliant. Sure, Historian A and I got off on the wrong foot the last time. So I must have just decided to completely forget my first experience with him, and I went at this event like the glass was half full. For now he and I are sharing a platform and we can discuss the pertinent issues, almost like – dare I say it – history buddies. Wait till he sees what an amazing person I am. He's so cool. And me? Okay, I'm not *as* cool, but I'm pretty sure I can be extremely engaging in a certain light and after a few drinks to a blind man on a galloping horse. It's a weekend, and I'm staying overnight, so I can see it all now – we'll be chatting and arguing all night about Cromwell. He'll mention *this* piece of evidence and I'll mention *that* piece of evidence. Well, this is just going to be an absolute hoot altogether.

I get to the appointed place, check into the hotel. There was some sort of a get-together in the hotel bar on the Friday evening. Don't ask me what. I can't remember. I didn't know anybody there, so I was dying to break the ice with all of these Cromwell buffs and see where the conversation went. I walk into the bar alone. I hate bars. Never drank in my life. So that didn't help. Wow. Look. A group of people are talking. There he is. Historian A. Right in the centre of them all. At the bar. It was like he was holding court. Watch this for a charm offensive. Oh, he's got his back turned. Cool. So, I move into his eyeline. He turns again. Hmm. I move into his eyeline again. He's talking about Cromwell. He turns again. I wanted to talk about Cromwell too. Aw janey mac, isn't this just brilliant?! I didn't have the confidence to interject, but I listened intently to what he was saying. At one point during the conversation he very obviously said something about the crass practice of just publishing books for the money and I could have sworn he looked in my direction. But I didn't really pick up on it at the time – it was only afterwards when I had time to reflect that it all came together. Anyway, I was far too excited to think that was even a thing. Nothing like a bit of banter between two budding bosom buddies.

But there was no banter. At least not between us.

Frustratingly I watched him incessantly turning as I tried in vain to catch his eye. What is it with the turning? Eventually I gave up and left Tina Turner to his machinations, chalked it up to bad luck, or poor social engagement on his part, and went to bed. Tomorrow in the cold light of day I'm sure I'll be able to get some face time with the man of the moment. Well, I hoped I would. I suppose it's possible that he could have read my book. Could he? Have read my book? Nah. Can't see it. Anyway, even if he *has* read it, wait until he sees me in full flow. How passionate I am about this. We'll be walking off into the sunset together linking arms yet. Just you wait and see.

My first big blow, as the actress said to the bishop

Saturday. Talk day. I enter the lecture auditorium. Getting a bit nervous now because I have to speak in front of a heap of people later, which I wasn't really that used to doing. At least I wasn't on until the afternoon. So I had the morning to listen to the other speakers. Okay, say nothing, there he is again. Now is your chance. I sidle up to the company he's in. Smiling inanely. Holy shit, he turns away again. Okay, so there's something not right here. There's no way this is a coincidence. If I could only get his attention, I'd prove that I was a nice guy and he really didn't have to keep turning away from me.

I watched him move through the room at a break in the morning talks. He was bound to come loose from one of his social clusters soon. Then it happened. He was on his own. It's now or never. I moved straight in front of him. There was no way he could turn away from me now. It was just me and him in the middle of the room. 'Hello, Historian A,' I said, calling him by his first name because he was bound to like that. Now that we were fellow speakers, sharing a podium, on a similar specialist topic. Let the foreplay begin. It was clearly a time to dispense with the formalities of Doctor This and Professor That. 'Are we okay, Historian A? You and me? You seem to be turning away from me a lot,' I blurted out – completely expecting him to apologise profusely, say he was mortified that I had gotten that impression from him, and rush out of the hotel to get me a box of Milk Tray as a peace offering.

His response was so shocking that afterwards I took the time to write down his disparaging words. I just didn't want to ever forget it. And I haven't. It went something like, 'You have no right to write anything about a subject you clearly know nothing about.' That was the gist of it. In fact it might well be those words verbatim. I didn't even have the strength to reach down and pull the virtual dagger from my chest. It was mortifying. I don't know what he was expecting me to say. I don't do confrontation. Debate, yes. Confrontation, no. Being the sensitive soul that I am, I was utterly devastated. It was a short conversation. Mortally wounded, I moved back to the sanctuary of my seat. I couldn't focus. My stomach was churning. I was in no way prepared for this. My rose-tinted glasses couldn't take the hit. I wanted my mammy. I had to bail. No way could I stay around here after that. And there's certainly no way I could do my talk. Not a hope. I was hurting very badly. You have to appreciate that these were the early days. I wasn't yet battle-hardened. That would eventually come. But to be belittled by my hero was just too much to take at that time.

My brilliant riposte – if I do say so myself

I found the organisers. 'I'm bailing,' I told the main woman.

She looked at me like I had two heads. 'What, why?' she asked, or something equally stirring.

I couldn't help myself. I was too young. Too naive. I told her the whole piece about Historian A. I simply couldn't pick myself up after the trauma. Yes, I was weak. I have no shame. I'm bailing. I have to. How could I go on after this?

But suddenly the prospect of letting these people down began to take a grip. I was in a serious jam. What am I doing? She doesn't deserve this. I can't simply walk away. What kind of a man am I? The kind that walks away from tricky situations? Well, yes, mostly that's true. But not today. I just couldn't. The lady was lovely. She gave me the choice. She said something like, 'That's completely understandable.' But all I heard was 'You total wuss. Are you for effen serious?'

So, now completely petrified of Historian A, and what he might say about my talk, as in like tear it to shreds in front of a live audience, I came up with a plan. 'Okay,' I said, 'I'll do it.' But I needed her to know something. If Historian A asked me any questions during the Q&A (there was to be a Q&A at the end, did I mention that?) I would refuse to answer him. Yep. I was *that* petulant. But that approach was certain to work on two levels. The second level will become obvious shortly. But the first one was that I wouldn't have to answer any of his questions about how wrong I was about stuff. Because there was no doubt, I *must* have been wrong about stuff, if he was adopting this hostile attitude to me.

The appointed moment arrived. I got up in front of the audience and told them that Cromwell didn't deliberately kill any civilians in Ireland during his time there. I watched jaws drop to the floor. Men shat themselves. Women wanted to batter me senseless. The only toddler in the room mooned at me. I even remember being so cocky that I told one shocked audience member she needed to 'get over it'. The lecture went well. At least its delivery. In fairness, the angry villagers' lynch mob must have been on their tea-break. Who knows, I might even have been emboldened by Historian A's verbal assault on me. Whatever it was I just got completely into the mode and gave it socks. Cromwell was a feckin saint! Boom! Suck it up. Most people in the room looked at me as if my lift didn't quite go to the top floor, but so far I was getting away with it.

Then came the Q&A. Historian A and the other speakers joined me on the stage. After some banal questions from the floor, one of Historian A's close academic associates blindsided me with attitude. 'What about Irish poetry?' he asked me. Apparently a lot of poetry confirmed Cromwell's guilt in this whole scenario. Who knew? Torn between wanting to laugh and being completely intrigued that this was clearly the stuff they discussed in universities, I dismissed his claim completely out of hand. Which is exactly what I would still do today. Poetry?! Holy crap. Is that what we're down to now? Depending on poetry to convict Cromwell of atrocities? Do me a favour.

Then it happened

Historian A looked across the stage at me and asked me a question. I guess he just couldn't help himself. 'In your book you say that there was a battle at Youghal. Can you tell us more about that battle please,' he asked. I'm paraphrasing but it was something along those lines. Of course, there was no battle at Youghal. I had completely misread the source that I had been researching. No surprise whatsoever to me. And excellent fodder for him. And as soon as he had the question out of his mouth, I knew that there was no such battle. I had it in my book, and I was wrong. But it was at this point that the self-assurance started to swell up inside me. I looked across at my former hero turned adversary and I couldn't believe he had fallen into my trap. I looked at the audience and I left a few seconds of a gap before answering – just to increase the tension.

Then I pushed the button

I said, 'I hoped this would not happen.' I found the organiser's eyes at the back of the room and I knew she was cringing. The mood in the room suddenly changed. 'I was hoping *you* would not ask me a question,' I continued. Of course, the fact that I had no answer to the question anyway and that I would be exposed as having made a mistake was not even a thing. This was my way out. 'This morning,' I began, looking intently at the audience, 'this man insulted me in a verbal attack, dismissing my work in a horrible way, and I have absolutely no intention of answering any of his questions. And I have told the organisers this already.'

It became deathly quiet. A tumbleweed rolled by. You could hear an early modern expert drop. For anyone who has ever attended a local history symposium, convention, conference, seminar, or even just a lecture, this is not the kind of shit that happens in that dusty, musty, stuffy old arena. I have no idea if Historian A squirmed much in front of the good people of that

European town somewhere in Europe that I daren't mention. But all I knew was that I had gained some sort of retribution. I felt like I had the high moral ground. I had exposed his unprovoked attack on me in the only way I knew how.

Keep your friends close and your Emilys closer still

But I learned a lesson that day. One that I would forget for the rest of my days, because that's what I do. Forget stuff. In essence, I had entered a world that I knew absolutely nothing about. And this experience was a complete eye-opener. Okay then, so we play dirty, do we? Okay, cool. I can do that.

Take that, Historian A. That was just the second time I had crossed swords with him. There would be others. But one thing was for sure: I had inadvertently made an opponent in the history business. Whether or not I had wanted one. And since he was such a big hitter, I knew that this did not augur well. I was already coming from a minus position. Did I mention that I got an F in history in the Leaving?

* Disclaimer: I have not revealed the identity of Historian A due to the fact that I suspect he would have quite a different slant on the events that I have described and the private conversation between us. This, after all, is simply my version of events, however imperfectly the passing years have influenced my recall. I'm old now and my memory is fading. So that's a thing. Any resemblance in the above to persons alive or dead must be purely the result of hallucinogenic weed or strong spirits. I don't smoke or drink so it must be you. I wouldn't need drugs anyway these days even if I had done them. I imagine I get the same effect now anyway just by standing up real fast.

Chapter 4

1999–2007

Frank

Now, I would have experienced the very same educational system that Drogheda Councillor Frank Godfrey would have gone through. Granted, Frank was older than me, but the Cromwell stories told to us in primary school of babies being nailed to church doors by Cromwell on an idle September afternoon would have given us all an inherent bias and a fierce hatred of that English See You Next Tuesday. Frank was brought up literally just yards from Scarlet Street in Drogheda. And as everybody with any connections to the town would know, Scarlet Street was the street where the blood of Cromwell's civilian victims was supposed to have run down in torrents, hence the name. This tradition is virtually intravenously administered into the arms of every babe in arms as soon as they are born above in the Lourdes Hospital. There was a local tradition, now long lost to the mists of time, that for years following the siege, Peter Street was called Bloody Street because of all the blood that was supposed to have run down the hill. The fact that Scarlet Street was outside the town walls at that time and that there were Scarlet streets and lanes in many towns throughout England and Ireland, including Dublin, in 1649 didn't really matter. It may well be the case that the word 'scarlet' has more to do with dyeing than dying. But just in case you're thinking of explaining this to somebody from Drawda, I wouldn't bother. They know better.

Frank has great pride in his town and is much respected by Droghedeans all over the world for the tireless work he does to make it a better place in which to live. Including yours truly.

Frank was about to enter this story from stage right. To be fair, I suspect he saw some votes in the stance that he took, and publicity he wanted, but few could have predicted the media storm that he and I were about to create when he decided to take me on. Okay, so it wasn't quite on the scale of one of those Kardashian-ass media storms, but it was big.

With the passing of the days, weeks and months after the book was published, loads of amazing things happened. Both Pat Kenny and Ryan Tubridy seemed to take me seriously and I really enjoyed my appearances on their shows. I was making waves. Making the news. The *Boston Herald* even ran a piece on the book. I just kept belting out the kernel of the thesis whenever I got the chance. Meanwhile, while I managed to convince some and shock many others with my abject treason, I was still waiting for some real historians to destroy my arguments. It was only a matter of time before an adult came into the room and told me to shut my face. Any day now.

Back in the parallel universe that was my real life, myself and the missus had somehow managed to convince the local St Mary's Church of Ireland Select Vestry to hand over their church to us so we could set up a heritage centre there. With dwindling attendances, they had already made the decision to deconsecrate the place and move their ceremonies to their more modern Julianstown complex. St Mary's Church of Ireland was the exact site where the breaches were made in the walls in 1649, and the old medieval churchyard had not changed a bit. The place reeks of history. We called it the Drogheda Heritage Centre and we opened in December 1999. It did not focus solely on Cromwell, but rather it interpreted the entire history of the town. But, ever the antagonist, I decided to try and market the place with a bit of controversy. Controversy sells. Didn't you know? The proof of that particular pudding was the fact that, according to Steve, my book was selling reasonably well.

Death mask divilment

This is where Frank comes in. During the research process for the book, I had discovered that there was something beyant in the UK called the Cromwell Association. Hmm. Interesting. I was already a member of the Old Drogheda Society and look where that had taken me. I was practically a legend in some parts of Drogheda now. So why not join this thing and see what I can find. Here was a core group of people who were so fascinated by this man that they sought to highlight the man's life and times in an association. Okay, they were mostly English, but I gave them the benefit of the doubt. All English people can't be complete hoors, can they? Can they? They didn't glorify the man as much as Frank seemed to think.

As we've already seen, it was more a promotion of a fascinating period of history where the English people had killed their own king and installed parliamentary rule in the first place and a Lord Protector in the second. And if you don't know already, you'd never guess who the Lord Protector turned out to be. Yep. You guessed it. The bould Ollie. It transpired that Frank heard the word Hitler whenever somebody mentioned the word Cromwell. In his eyes, I had joined the Hitler Association. Fair dinkum. I get that. I would have probably been there before I started on this crusade. But the Cromwell Association was just about as toxic as the innocuous and not-at-all-sinister Old Drogheda Society. In, like, not at all. It was a humdrum old historic society. End of.

Anyway, as the only Irish member of the association, no doubt I caused a wee ripple among the existing members. I also got to know John Goldsmith, who was Mister Cromwell Association to me, but in real life he was the curator of the Cromwell Museum in Huntingdon. Through John I became aware that a death mask of the quare fella had been made in the days after his death in 1658 and it still existed. So, me being me,

I asked John if I could have the lend of this mask for display in our new heritage centre. John agreed and had the mask sent to us. Cue the mayhem.

Hitler becomes a thing

I then conceived this hilariously titled advertising campaign that I called 'He's Back! Cromwell Returns to Drogheda'. I knew it would freak a lot of people out, and that was the entire objective, but I didn't bank on Frank. The *Drogheda Independent* ran a story on the exhibition and that was enough for the intrepid councillor, who had recently become the deputy mayor, to completely lose his shit. He had reached breaking point. Arriving at the recently opened centre one morning, I was faced with a group of protestors holding up placards. There was the deputy mayor at their head. It was the quintessential 'Down with this sort of thing' moment. Straight out of *Father Ted*. 'Not Cromwellcome' shouted one of the signs in an attempt at a clever pun that just didn't quite hit the mark for me. And I love wordplay! 'Drogheda says no to Cromwell devil mask' screamed another. One of the protestors had daubed tomato juice on the walls of the graveyard to represent the blood of the civilians that Cromwell clearly slaughtered according to the demonstrators. The *Irish Mirror* actually dedicated several pages to the controversy in different editions over a few weeks. In one full-page piece Frank bizarrely challenged me to a duel and we were both depicted in duelling garb from the seventeenth century. So weird.

'Cromwell was an evil man who slaughtered our people and it's an insult to bring his death mask here,' said Frank. 'I've said it before and I'll say it again: bringing Cromwell to Drogheda is like bringing Hitler to the Jews. Revisionists are trying to say that the massacres never happened, but it's the same as saying that the Holocaust never happened,' he insisted.

Grr. There's that Hitler thing again. I should get used to that, I suppose. It's always gonna be a default argument for many. Well, this was a turn-up for the books.

Getting up on my high horse

The publicity that we got from this was totally unprecedented. A veritable blitz ensued. Local papers and radio stations did their thing. National papers and radio stations did the same. We even ended up in the *Observer*. But *Ireland AM* on TV3 was probably the highlight for me. Frank and I were asked to appear on the morning show and debate the issues. We did. It was great. Naturally, in my own head I won. Frank probably had other ideas. He always did. Once I got a taste of fame, I was hooked. Some people may have thought I was in this for the money. My ass. There's no money in books. Certainly not in the kind of books I write. Ten per cent of the retail price? Two thousand books? And God knows how long it would take to sell them all, if at all. I never even considered the money. For me this was all about getting my message out there. I had a battle to fight. I was David. The might of academia was Goliath. The more exposure the topic got, the more exposure my thesis would get. That's the way I saw it. If I'm right, the message really needs to get through to the masses.

Boy, was I naive

What I was basically saying was something that, if I was right, oodles of academics who studied the period for years had completely missed. Not just in Ireland. Internationally. Now c'mon, people. Do I have to mention my exam results again? How likely was that exactly? This tradition was so embedded in the Irish psyche that the task of undoing centuries of legacy and tradition seemed completely impossible. But boy was I going to try. As far as I could make out, this was a humongous miscarriage of historical justice. Cromwell was not to blame for the deliberate indiscriminate civilian deaths, and that was simply wrong. From this point onwards I felt I was promoting a noble cause. Trying to right a wrong. I was Atticus Finch in *To Kill a Mocking Bird*. Henry Fonda (who cares what his character's name was) in *Twelve Angry Men*, Andy Dufresne in *The Shawshank Redemption*, Grumpy in *Snow White and the Seven Dwarves*.

The local media had the controversy going on for weeks, to the point where a local wag even wrote a poem about all the shenanigans and a cartoon was drawn by a newspaper cartoonist for the greater public's delectation. Frank did loads of stuff in the background, including making massive efforts to discredit my book. He made several calls for the British government to apologise for Cromwell's actions in Ireland just to see if that would gain traction. It didn't. They were probably very busy with real issues at the time.

Shitting myself on RTE's *Sunday Show*

I was even invited to go on Andy O'Mahony's *Sunday Show* on RTE Radio 1. Now, I wouldn't have been part of the *Sunday Show* audience. But I high-tailed it to the studio in Donnybrook in good time, anticipating more plaudits as the star of the show and blowing the country away with my erudition. Was there no end to my media exploits?

Unfortunately, the researcher didn't tell me that it was a panel show.

I had never either heard the show or, worse still, heard *of* the show so I had no clue. When three other guests sat down around the table, I shat myself. I realised that they were going to be talking about the pertinent issues of the day and I was expected to contribute as a panel member. So not only was I supposed to have an opinion, but it was supposed to be an insightful opinion.

Well, they have their shite. Nobody mentioned any panel to me. Bastards. How dare they assume the whole world knew what the *Sunday Show* was. The arrogance.

So, instead of embracing the moment, I sat there like an idiot fuming at being put in this position and I said absolutely nothing. Not a thing. Andy was perplexed. I was freaked. It was all politics. Mostly about the North. I had nothing. No way was I going to make a complete fool of myself. I watched Andy look at me for a reaction to stuff, but I remained completely silent. I was of course completely petrified. I think Andy realised I had frozen. Not like me at all. But this was not my area. No way Josie. I figured they'd have to bring the death mask controversy up at some stage since they'd asked me on. Andy copped that I was struggling, so after a respectable amount of time he engaged me fully in a conversation about Cromwell. Looking back on it now he was probably scared shitless that I'd stay totally frozen.

But I stunned Andy like a wind-up doll by coming completely to life. Naturally, I was completely brilliant. Cromwell was my thing. I was as articulate and effusive as a politician on speed. As soon as the Cromwell conversation finished, I returned to being the village idiot. I said nothing right to the end of the programme. Not sure that I got away with that one. Oddly, years later, since my name was clearly on their list, and as they must have been stuck for guests, a researcher called me up one day and asked me as a former panelist if I would like to go on again. Once bitten. Not a fricken hope, pet. True story.

Another blow from another historian. What gives?

Picking up the *Drogheda Independent* during this entire debacle was done with some trepidation. My fears were to be realised when a letter from the eminent historian Pádraig Lenihan of the University of Limerick appeared one week. 'I disagree with author Reilly's interpretation of what happened,' was the headline. And sure enough the sub-editor had gotten it right as the following words in the letter seem to prove: 'I must say that I do not agree with Tom's interpretation of what happened in Drogheda in September 1649. So innocent civilians were killed. How many? It would be dangerous to speculate on the basis of the town's pre and post-war...I would tentatively suggest about a thousand civilians,' wrote my latest antagonist.

Janey mac. Another push-back from an expert in the history business! What's going on? But there was one thing missing – evidence. I took particular note of Pádraig's word 'speculate'. And I thought to myself at that time: okay, so speculation again, eh? Well, that's just *his* opinion. Granted, the man sleeps, eats and drinks the seventeenth century. But in my experience, opinions are potentially changeable. The truth of the fact is beyond argument. And Pádraig didn't present any solid facts to support his case. So I got over that hurdle by deciding that he was entitled to his opinion, as was I. I wasn't in the least bit fazed. He might well disagree, but he hasn't convinced me that I was in any way mistaken. I was pretty sure that day would come. But it hadn't arrived just yet. Phew. That was a close one.

Every day's a school day

Then in 2002 a strange thing happened. I was alerted to the fact that I featured heavily in an English schoolbook entitled *Presenting the Past* by Andrew Wrenn and Keith Worrall. An English schoolbook by jingo! The book was published by HarperCollins, no less. Nothing but the best, you understand. There I was in full living colour across a two-page spread covering pages 64 and 65.

'This is Tom Reilly,' gushed the narrative. 'Tom is an Irish historian [aw, Jaysus – I am *not* a historian!] who was born in Drogheda. He was brought up on tales of Cromwell's cruelty. But Tom wasn't happy about what he was told. He wanted to find out the *real* story of Cromwell's time in Ireland. This is what he found out about what Cromwell did at Drogheda...and at Wexford.'

The book goes on to explain that I proposed the notion that none of Drogheda's unarmed civilians had been deliberately killed by the New Model Army. Well, this was exciting stuff. It would only be a matter of time before Irish schoolbooks were doing the same. Wouldn't it? Be only a matter of time? My bollix. That won't happen in my feckin' lifetime. Tradition dies very hard in this neck of the woods.

Historian B joins the fun

I think it's probably about time I introduced you to Historian B. While I'm doing my best to tell the story chronologically, between imperfect memory recall and efforts to make the story as charming as possible, I may end up taking some minor liberties in the narrative timeline. So, if you're Historian B, then you'll probably recognise yourself as Dr Jason McElligott.

I first encountered McElligott when I picked up his book *Cromwell: Our Chief of Enemies*. Jason clearly likes wordplay as well, because his title was a play on the words *Cromwell: Our Chief of Men*, which is the title of Antonia Fraser's epic biography on Cromwell, and which in turn was taken from a poem also about Cromwell by John Milton. And now that I've mentioned this particular tome, I am delighted to reveal that this was absolutely and categorically the book that began my change of mind about the auld bollix. Fraser's – not McElligott's. I was completely beguiled by Lady Antonia's incredible narrative. I would wholeheartedly encourage the world and its mother to read this book. Because in these pages is the real Oliver Cromwell. His personality is brilliantly extracted from seventeenth-century documents, mainly his letters and speeches and parliamentary papers. And in this book, I could find no monster. Instead I found a man of paradoxes, a man of contradictions, but in the main an honourable, or dare I say it, an admirable man. There, I've said it.

But back to McElligott. When I realised that he had come to Drogheda to research his book, I was a little put out that he didn't make an effort to contact me, so I could make things easier for him as he navigated the town and this Cromwell thing. After all, I was the local Cromwell expert. I wrote to him to praise his book and also to uproariously mention that he really should have contacted me but that I'd let him off with it because I was that nice. See? Fun-ny.

I was genuinely just trying to open up a dialogue with a similarly minded individual, as I saw it back then. In those days I simply looked up the telephone book, found a McElligott in there and posted an actual letter in an actual postbox with an actual stamp. Letters. Ah, bless. Thing of the past now. Remarkably it reached him.

Anyway, at some point in these proceedings, McElligott decided to run an evening course on Cromwell in what was then known as UCD (University College Dublin). Well, as soon as I heard that, I signed up straight away. A course on Cromwell? The course was interesting, but after two sessions I bailed. Again, I had thought I had found a kindred spirit because the guy was a complete expert on Cromwell. But in hindsight Jason was never gonna contact me when he was writing his book because I was an amateur, or for whatever reason he didn't. (That chip on my shoulder was getting bigger and bigger at that time. You should see it now.) And what was the point? There was something rotten in the State of Bismarck. I was starting to realise that professional historians may have had a thing about amateurs. And it wasn't good. Or was it just the historians that *I* was finding out there in the history wuddled? Irrespective, of course, that only emboldened me up the effen wazoo.

Holy crap – he buys the Wood bullshit

During the course I felt like I was cramping his style by even being in the room. McElligott and I differed significantly on some fundamental issues. It could be summed up in three words: 'massacred unarmed civilians'. There is a piece of evidence that he was completely buying, but I wasn't. It was from a guy called Thomas à Wood, who was a Cromwellian soldier and is said to have fought with Cromwell at Drogheda. Wood provided specific details on the killing of the defenceless inhabitants. And in Jason's view there was no arguing with a Cromwellian soldier who actually witnessed the events and left us an account of what happened. But I either wasn't that gullible, or that nationalistic. I could never work out which. But more about Mr Wood anon.

It was around this time too that I realised that people's political views seemed to colour their assessment of these particular events. If you had republican leanings in any way at all, and you hated or even disliked the Brits for the 800 years of oppression, you were absolutely bound to believe Cromwell was a murdering See You Next Tuesday. It didn't make any difference what facts might be out there. No point in ruining a good story with facts. I got the distinct impression that even if time travel was a thing, I could take the dissenters back to Drogheda on 11 September 1649, stop off for a cappuccino, show them what actually happened in full living colour, and they still wouldn't believe me.

Ouch! Ouch! Ouch! For Chrissake stop it, Jason!

Anyway, McElligott completely went for me in a review of my book that he posted on Amazon.com. McElligott says:

> This is a remarkable attempt to revise the accepted view of Cromwell in Ireland. For Reilly, a native of Drogheda, Cromwell was an honourable soldier who did not cause

the death of a single unarmed civilian in his hometown. In Reilly's account Cromwell is a reasoned, enlightened 'humanitarian' who has been the victim of his enemy's black propaganda. This is a startling thesis which, if it were true, would put generations of historians to shame. It would be easy to ridicule Reilly's dreadful prose; his enthusiastic description of the McDonald's outlet in modern Drogheda will, unfortunately, remain with me for a very long time. Yet, the main weaknesses of this book are not stylistic, but historical. To be blunt, *Cromwell: An Honourable Enemy* owes more to Reilly's often expressed desire to 'rehabilitate the memory of Cromwell in Ireland' than it does to any generally accepted rules of historical practice.

The author exhibits a profound unfamiliarity with the history of the English Revolution of the mid-seventeenth century. Furthermore, Reilly has chosen to write about perhaps the most controversial period of Irish history without consulting a single book or pamphlet dating from the time of the sack of Drogheda. Instead, he bases his thesis on extracts of contemporary sources reproduced, with varying degrees of accuracy, in the nineteenth and twentieth centuries. As such, he makes a number of serious blunders, the most important of which concerns Cromwell's letter to the House of Commons after the battle at Drogheda. The original letter does not survive but the official printed version confirms that 'many inhabitants' were among those killed by Cromwell's forces at Drogheda. If this pamphlet is authentic, Reilly's thesis is in ruins.

Reilly asserts that there is no contemporary evidence for the massacre of civilians at Drogheda. At times one cannot but feel something approaching admiration for Reilly's ability to deal from the bottom of the deck, but one cannot get away from the fact that he has done too little research to support his extravagant claims. He is completely unaware of John Evelyn's diary entry for 15 September 1649 which tells how he received 'news of Drogheda being taken by the Rebells and all put to the sword.' Neither is he familiar with a report in a newspaper named *Mercurius Elencticus*, dated 15 October 1649, which tells how the Cromwellians at Drogheda 'possessed themselves of the Towne, and used all crueltie imaginable upon the besieged, as well inhabitants as others, sparing neither women nor children.' Had Reilly been aware of these sources he would, undoubtedly, have found some grounds to dismiss them, but when they are read in conjunction with the numerous other accounts of civilian deaths at Drogheda there can be no doubt about what happened in that town in September 1649. This is, in short, a painfully bad book.

That was pretty ouchy. Yep, things weren't going so well any more. I really wanted a historian to agree with me. Someone somewhere. Anyone! Jason McElligott was yet another seventeenth-century historian who was well respected and was extremely familiar with his subject. And there he was, dissin' me like a bad-ass gangsta. I suppose he thought that mentioning Cromwell's letter was a good point. But I had an answer to that, in the same way that I had an answer to everything McElligott was likely to throw at me.

Duck! Incoming!

A review in *History Ireland* at this same time by one Eugene Coyle was also a swift kick in the nads:

The historical evidence presented by Reilly is not convincing. The author's style is often superficial, volatile, tendentious and partisan in the face of known historical evidence. The book adds little to our understanding of the actions of Cromwell at Drogheda or at Wexford. There is a need for a new book on the Irish Cromwellian campaign but unfortunately this is not it.

Hmm. That was odd. He finished with the same flourish that Kevin Whelan had finished his review with in the *Irish Times*. Still, it was also pretty damning. But I was still completely getting off on the reviews from Charles Chevenix Trench and Ruth Dudley Edwards, and if I could convince *them*, then I really might be on to something here. But obviously there is a lot more work to do yet.

Watch out, David (that's me BTW) – here comes Goliath!

And so, I looked to my friends in the Cromwell Association for affirmation. John Morrill was President of the Cromwell Association and is arguably the foremost historian in the world when it comes to Oliver Cromwell. Engaging in some e-mail correspondence with the great man, I received an e-mail from him that went something like this: 'Have I ever actually said that I am totally convinced by your evidence that no civilians died in cold blood at Drogheda? I am not quite so clear that some would not have been caught up in the crossfire and hot blood. But your careful re-reading of all of the evidence about Cromwell's campaign I find convincing.'

Well, that's good. At least I have John Morrill on my side. A titan in the world of Cromwell. So, you can imagine my surprise some years later (2007) when I read his article 'The Drogheda Massacre in Cromwellian Context', in the book *Age of Atrocity*, where he writes:

Jason McElligott has given us an outstanding summary of the nationalist and revisionist cases and a totally convincing and necessary explanation of why Tom Reilly's claim that there was no civilian massacre at Drogheda is not to be trusted. In essence Reilly fails the test of source criticism at almost every turn. He argues a case and unreasonably privileges second- and third-hand evidence that supports his presupposition and unreasonably dismisses contrary evidence. When it comes to first-hand evidence, he reasserts an already discredited attempt to deny that Cromwell confessed to the deaths of civilians...And what does this appendix tell us? It tells us that at Drogheda Cromwell's army killed 60 royalist officers, 220 troopers, and 2,500 infantry, surgeons, 'and many inhabitants'. There is no getting around these words. Reilly tries to do so...by drawing attention to Carlyle's false claim in the first edition of [*Letters and Speeches*] that the appendix is an eighteenth-century addition...this claim was simply incorrect. This in itself is fatal to Reilly's thesis and it is disgraceful that so many reviewers have not checked this. Despite Tom Reilly's attempt to minimise the number of civilian deaths, there can be no doubt that they took place.

We'll deal with the details contained in Morrill's quote in the next chapter, if you can stay awake until then. But for now, it looks to me like the historians closed ranks for some reason. Some of them, like Morrill, took a while to get the message to disparage me. He mustn't have been at the original meeting. Or he might have missed the Post-It note. At one stage in the debate McElligott called me pugnacious, which was fair enough. If the cap fits. Guilty, your honour. And I have a feeling that the reason many historians dismiss my work wholesale is something to do with me shooting my mouth off on a regular basis. You know, pugnacious. I don't fart, walk, talk or act like a historian. Why would I? I'm not one! *Capisce?* But what choice do I have now? I simply gotta fight this. I've got right on my side. I'm standing up for the little fella. And I don't mean Cromwell. I mean amateur historians all over the world. These professional feckers don't seem to want to accept that a complete amateur can change a perception of history that they clearly missed. Especially this controversial one. The historians have spoken. How could anyone question the historians?

Well, just watch me!

Chapter 5

2007–2008

Feckin' keyboard warriors

The online abuse started early. Even though it was pre-Facebook, there were plenty of websites and blogs that threw large doses of vitriol at me. While it wasn't something I had been prepared for, I got used to it pretty quickly. I don't have a political bone in my body and I genuinely couldn't care less who's in government at any given time. To me, they're all extremely clever people who do their best for their country. And they were savvy enough to get elected, because that's a tough gig. Although, wasn't there something about Charlie Haughey that didn't quite ring true? Anyway, point being – I was not coming at this from any political perspective. It was when I started getting nasty comments from nationalists and republicans who had the tricolor as a backdrop to their profile pics that I realised that one's politics somehow determined how one would view this Cromwell and Ireland issue. The Irish Americans called me everything under the sun. Feckin' loons. No offence, folks. I mean – no offense, folks.

I never fully understood why the following happened, but I just let it happen anyway because it seemed like a good thing to me. Steve contacted me in 2000 and told me that he had done a deal with UK company, the Orion Publishing Group, who were going to reissue the book under their imprint, the Phoenix Press. It was going to be a softback. So, sales must have been going well. 'Knock yourself out,' I said and got straight back up on the horse and into the fray again.

Saints preserve us!

Now, we've already mentioned my relationship with the Catholic religion, the dogma of which I had completely railed against, as

I discovered the cesspit of depravity it had been throughout the centuries – and other stories. So you can imagine my reaction when in June 2001 I read an article in the local paper, the headline of which read, 'Campaign on behalf of five priests put to death by Cromwell – Now is the time to pray for their beatification.' The one-sided article freaked me out as it said things like, 'These martyrs died without hatred in their hearts...Cromwell's way of dealing with them was summary execution.' Not a mention of the reasons Cromwell disliked the political movement that was the Catholic faith, an organisation that slaughtered millions of innocent souls because they would not conform to their faith. Not a mention of the fact that Catholic priests are documented as having stirred the Irish into rebellion in 1641, which caused the deaths of about 5,000 innocent Protestants. Not a mention of the fact that one of these priests at Drogheda was prepared to deny his faith by masquerading as a soldier. Nothing. It was all 'Catholics equals good. Cromwell equals bad.' What a load of shite.

Of course I caused more consternation locally when I wrote to the paper challenging this nonsense. The editor gave my letter the heading, 'Sainthood – dubious grounds'. Of course, all this did was alienate me further from local religious nut jobs, which was becoming par for the course. Now I'm a Cromwell-loving Catholic-hating looper, and that was enough for some people to take me off their dinner party guest lists. Thanks be to Jaysus for small mercies!

An Bullán

Elsewhere, poor Jason McElligott just couldn't let it lie. He decided to take his best shot. In an article that was published in *An Bullán* in 2001 entitled 'Cromwell, Drogheda and the Abuse of Irish History' he completely went for me. I reckon it's important to repeat a good chunk of what he wrote in that article so now it can come back to bite him on the ass. It's in print. So I'm not exaggerating it in any way at all. Good man, Jason. I wonder if you're reading this. Bet you are. Enjoying it so far? Excellent. Well, here's what you wrote back in 2001. Remember it?

The most vocal and pugnacious of the Drogheda Revisionists is Tom Reilly, a businessman and native of the town who has set himself the Herculean task of 'rehabilitating the memory of Cromwell in Ireland.' Reilly's first book on the subject, *Cromwell at Drogheda* (1993), was relatively restrained. In it he dismissed Thomas Wood's account of his involvement in the killing of women and children at Drogheda and claimed that without this testimony 'the evidence against Cromwell and the slaughter of innocents is decidedly weak.' In 1999, however, Reilly produced a much more ambitious book with the deliberately provocative title of *Cromwell: An Honourable Enemy*. In this work Reilly constructs an image of Cromwell as an honourable soldier who did not cause the death of a single unarmed civilian in the town.

Cromwell: An Honourable Enemy has sold seventy thousand copies, received the praise of prominent historians, and, on the back of his success, Reilly has become something of a regular on radio and television in Britain and Ireland. It is, therefore, important to analyse Reilly's book and establish whether this remarkable thesis has any basis in fact. It is my contention not merely that this book is fatally flawed from beginning to end, but that the praise heaped upon it by certain sections of the media and the historical profession tells us something both interesting and profoundly disturbing about contemporary Irish society and its attitude towards the past.

To be frank, Reilly's book owes more to his personal enthusiasm for the memory of Oliver Cromwell than it does to any generally accepted rules of historical practice. The author exhibits a profound unfamiliarity with the history of the English Revolution of the mid-seventeenth century.

Indeed, *Cromwell: An Honourable Enemy* is such a painfully bad book that were it not for the rave reviews it has received in some quarters, such a lengthy deconstruction of the text might seem like taking a sledgehammer to crack a nut.

A number of reviewers have taken issue with Reilly's claims, but in general the book has received a warm reception in Ireland. Part of the explanation for this reception is the enthusiasm of the revisionists for anything that attacks the nationalist interpretation of history. Yet the enthusiasm of some historians for Reilly's book would not in itself be a cause for alarm; much of the large readership of history in Ireland is skeptical of the wilder excesses of the revisionists. The main factor that has led to the favourable reaction to *Cromwell: An Honourable Enemy* is the rapidly changing nature of Irish society. Many people in modern Ireland are uncomfortable with the often-grubby realities of Irish history. They wish to project an image of a sophisticated and cosmopolitan European country. In this context, Reilly's bold reassessment of the greatest bogey-man in Irish history has a superficial appeal. This new-found willingness to re-examine the past is commendable but the rush to adopt any theory, so long as it sounds 'modern' and 'sophisticated,' demonstrates the parochial and unsophisticated nature of much of what passes for informed comment in Ireland. All the evidence suggests that Cromwell slaughtered the garrison and many of the townspeople of Drogheda in September 1649. In doing so he stepped outside the norms of seventeenth century warfare. To pretend otherwise is an abuse of Irish history.

So much scorn from one so young. You'd wonder where it was all coming from. The best thing about Jason's review was that he insisted on calling me a businessman. YES! Is it *that* hard? I didn't want to be called a historian! Of course, Jason may have meant it in a patronising way because that's the only way it fits into his negative narrative. But the cap fits. And I was so happy to wear it. Also, I think he might have inadvertently complimented me and called the book 'modern' and 'sophisticated'.

Shit, Jason, if you thought my prose was bad in my earlier books, you won't be able to cope with this current narrative you're presently reading. Not very history-esque, eh?

Well, despite what you might think, that article was water off a duck's back. The sledgehammer to crack a nut analogy was soooo interesting. What he was basically saying was that he had evidence that resembled a sledgehammer and that it could be used to crack my evidence that resembled a nut. And that my nut would be completely pummelled to oblivion. (Insert nut joke here.) Unfortunately, despite having the opportunity to do so in this article, Jason didn't use his...erm...sledgehammer. He didn't even use his nutcracker.

I have no idea where Jason got his misinformation on my book sales. Seventy thousand! I'm guessing that it wasn't from Nielsen, the people who actually have accurate totals on book sales. I don't even think it was *seven* thousand. But in one fell swoop, by the mistake in the typo I was suddenly an author of significant repute. *Seventy thousand* copies. I could get a good lot of mileage out of this one. Anyway, however adamant he seems to have been, Jason's rebuttals could be very easily rebutted, and I will get to that shortly. Isn't it great that people can just write what they like and just leave it there for years for the world to see, much like I'm doing here really. It's called living in a democracy.

Is that gobshite on the telly again?

The telly thing that Jason was talking about was great. In 2001 I had been contacted by UK documentary company Wall to Wall Productions. They were making a film entitled *Cromwell: New Model Englishman* – and they wanted my input. Yey! I was gonna be on telly. Hollywood, here I come! This was brilliant! I gave them what they wanted. Couldn't get enough of the camera. It was great making the contribution because now I had espoused my theory on national TV. That should put the cat among the pigeons.

The following year I was contacted by another English documentary maker. Cromwell had been voted as one of the top ten Britons in BBC 2's quest to establish who the Greatest Briton in history was. They had a top 100 that included Bob Geldof and Bono (unreal, I know), but a documentary was to be made of all the top ten, and the people of Britain would vote for their winner. Military historian Richard Holmes was going to present the film on Cromwell. They came to Drogheda, interviewed me, and sent the film out into the world. For the record, Winston Churchill was eventually voted as the Greatest Briton ever. Between books, magazines and websites, several things happened to affirm my position as a Cromwell apologist. It was so reassuring to see the impact I was making, albeit a modest one. So, it wasn't all bad. And of course, the more my work seemed to be accepted, the more emboldened I became as the time passed. With every passing day I was waiting for the first serious challenge from some historian somewhere to shut me up. Yet, as the weeks were passing, there was no real sign of it. It was early days though, in all fairness.

'Only recently have Irish historians like Tom Reilly had the scholarly integrity to get the story right,' said Simon Schama in his *History of Britain*. Hey Simon! Thanks, but I am *not* a historian! Can you people please stop calling me a bloody historian! This is becoming a real pain in the ass now. I've made every feckin' effort to emphasise that I'm just a chancer. Where's the real story behind this if people think I'm actually a historian? Historians can change a perception of history. It's their job. Chancers can't. Chancers don't. How many times do I gotta say it?!

Getting into some of the deets

I suppose at some stage in this narrative I should probably outline some of the things that I discovered along the way. As I delved deeper into the mire of seventeenth-century politics I realised that it's an extremely complicated period in Irish and British history. Did that deter me? Did it feck. Not in the least. Might as well be hung for a leep as a shamb. What difference could it possibly make that I was a complete novice at this history stuff? Sure, everything was complicated when it came to history, wasn't it? To me history was just like a big fruit cake, full of dates.

Suffice to say my idea of wiping the slate clean turned out to be a douzy. And by that, I mean I decided to completely shed my anti-English conditioning. But even that wasn't enough. At the same time, I became highly tuned in to the fact that most people who wrote about this topic over the centuries usually displayed a bias. One way or the other. But mostly against Ollie. Naturally. Even English writers seemed to be suggesting that he completely lost control on Irish soil and simply slipped back into his role as Mr Congeniality when he returned to England. So, anything that was written after 1660 was essentially not worth paying any attention to. The main reason for this was the fact that when Ollie died, his son, Tumbledown Dick (which is not an early contraceptive made out of duck feathers as it turns out) made a complete pig's mickey out of being head-of-state. In 1660 the monarchy was restored. And at that stage not only did the truth become a casualty, it had the shite completely beaten out of it and was left for dead. It was open season on Cromwell and his republic and there wasn't a thing he could do about it. That was mainly because he was well dead. History is written by the winners, said Confucius, or somebody equally clever back in the day. And he or she was right.

'Spud' Murphy

It became clear to me as the time passed that the education I had received was heavily influenced by late nineteenth-century literature. There were many others, but in particular I'm talking about that book that was written in 1883 by a Father Denis Murphy, a Catholic priest, called *Cromwell in Ireland* that I had bought in Kenny's of Galway. As a cleric, Dinny went for Ollie's jugular. He totally excoriated the nads off him. And at a time when we were being asked to become a nation once again, this fitted the victim narrative perfectly for Irish men and women everywhere. All the more reason to simply go back to the documents that were written at the time – in the actual year 1649.

As the flow cries, these events aren't really that long ago. If the average person lives to the age of 80 these days, and if you allow for inflation, take away the number you first thought of – we're only talking about five or six generations back. Okay, seven then. So, what I'm saying is this isn't exactly the Dark Ages. (Wasn't the Dark Ages called that because there were just too many knights around? Somebody stop me!) It was also a time of some literary proficiency as well. About 30 per cent of the population could write. There were many participants in the wars who wrote their own accounts of their experiences. To me, this was the crock of gold, the hub, the kernel, the nucleus from which the key information should come. And this is where I decided to concentrate my efforts.

Believe Wood? I Wood in me arse

For *Honourable Enemy*, I compiled an eyewitness and non-eyewitness list of those who wrote stuff about the storming of Drogheda. There's no real need to go into any great detail of that here, because I've already done that elsewhere. In the book, you idiot! Sheesh. So now we come to the evidence of Thomas à Wood, the royalist turned Cromwellian soldier who fought with Cromwell at Drogheda and who gave us the only details of civilian deaths that we have today. And just before we get into this it's probably worth saying that Jason buys this Wood 'evidence' sook, line and hinker.

At the time I thought that there was little doubt that young Thomas Wood witnessed the events. (More about this anon.) The story that he tells us surrounds a beautifully dressed and bejewelled girl whom the attacking soldiers came across on the streets of Drogheda. Naturally Wood himself tried to save her initially, but apparently one of his mates came up and just stabbed her in the belly, so they just robbed her jewels and threw her over the wall. Like you do. Wood also told stories of local children being grabbed and held up as human shields to save the attacking soldiers from being 'shot or brained'. Now this was a piece of evidence that was very difficult to argue with. It seemed to fly in the face of Cromwell's own words that he did not harm the hair on the head of any man when he said, 'Give us an instance of one man, not in arms, massacred, destroyed or banished.' Of course, Cromwell could easily have just been a complete liar. Remember Comical Ali? Then there's Putin. Everything he says is a lie. But Wood was an eyewitness (allegedly) and as an ordinary Cromwellian soldier what possible motive did he have to say such things?

As it happens, I didn't have to look far to see his evidence being discredited. In a bookshop in Cambridge, on one of my visits there, I picked up Samuel Rawson Gardiner's *The Commonwealth and The Protectorate*. Sammy made a few daycent points about Wood's account. Firstly, he wondered how likely it was that a girl would dress in her finest clothes, put all her jewels on her and go for a walk on the streets of the town during a manic bloodbath. Not a great argument really, though. No real point in taking Wood's statement so literally, I thought. He also highlighted that, of course, Wood himself tried to make himself out to be chivalrous at first. Hmm. Still not brilliant. But then Sammy came out with a belter. He had done his research and he had discovered a quote from Wood's commanding officer who described him as a buffoon who used to tell jokes all the time. Okay I'm paraphrasing, but you get the gist. And as far as Sammy was concerned, this was just the kind of guy who would make up lurid stories to titillate an audience. So, at that time, that was enough for me. I completely embraced Sammy Gardiner's interpretation of Wood's narrative. But in truth, it continued to niggle away at me over the years and I wondered if I was simply just trying to make this piece of evidence suit my agenda. Because it did.

Those who live by the sword spin by the sword

With our heritage centre struggling badly, and following the amazing publicity levels we reached for displaying Cromwell's death mask, I put my thinking cap on. I found out that the actual sword that Cromwell used to cut my ancestors' todgers off at Drogheda was still in existence. So why not? In August 2002 I simply made up the story that we were preparing to display the fecker's sword, the actual one that did all the damage, and I sent it out in a press release. I was aware that the sword itself was in the Royal Armouries in Leeds, but I didn't bother asking them for a loan of it because I figured I didn't actually need it. Anyway, the media took the bait, and they printed the story. Another mini blitz happened with local people taking sides. Frank of course went mad, but on this occasion the Old Drogheda Society supported my endeavours.

'The sword is symbolic of the bloody massacre of people in Drogheda,' said Frank in the *Daily Mirror*, 5 July 2002. 'The people of Drogheda will never forget the massacre of the townspeople in 1649.' It was a win-win situation for me.

I simply said that I'd decided to cancel the exhibition because of the adverse publicity. Pretty good, eh?

I'm sorry. I'm sorry. I'm sorry

Then as the months passed and I was chillin' with my homies, getting on with whatever it was I did for a living, in September 2003 I read an odd story in the *Drogheda Independent*. The headline read, 'Cromwell Apology'. The piece read:

> There may be controversy over whether or not the Oliver Cromwell massacre of Drogheda was fact or myth but locals from his hometown of Huntingdon are set to officially apologise for his actions.

Holy mother of the divine shite! It went on:

> Arise Ministries are planning to do a reconciliation walk entitled 'Cromwell's Steps' and will be bringing letters of repentance and apology from Huntingdon Town Council.

It gets even worse.

On their arrival in town the same paper reported:

> The group visiting Drogheda this week from Oliver Cromwell's hometown of Huntingdon do so, it has been claimed, with a letter of support from the British Prime Minister, Tony Blair.

Oh, for God's sake. Jesus, Mary and Holy Saint Joseph!

Here was I, wanting the Irish people to apologise to the Cromwell family for blackening his name all these years and here come these people wanting to apologise for what he did – or more importantly what he didn't do – to us!

Frank was on cloud nine. At last, somebody who actually understood his pain. Somebody who understood that all of the people of Drogheda were slaughtered by this bloodthirsty maniac.

'Their apology to the people of Drogheda for the actions of Cromwell against our forefathers on behalf of the people of Huntingdon is a magnanimous expression of goodwill and reconciliation,' he said.

In response I was reported as saying:

There seems to be widespread ignorance surrounding the events at Drogheda in 1649 if residents of Huntingdon think an apology is necessary. Not one man died for the cause of Irish nationalism at Drogheda. But there was no shortage of those who died for their precious English king.

I then wrote a letter to the paper (I wrote a lot of letters back in those days) and I was surprised that the editor actually published it. And it went something like this:

Dear Sir,

I am trying to put a group together to officially apologise for something, but I'm not sure exactly what. But I suppose we could officially apologise to the Vikings for the town of Drogheda not being built when they arrived. To the Normans for the damp local weather. To all of the provincial towns in Ireland for getting the Pope to visit here when they couldn't. For having the head of Oliver Plunkett when they don't. And for hogging the mouth of the Boyne when they can't. Hang on, I know. Why don't we officially apologise to the people of Huntingdon because their English king's army killed Cromwell's men at the siege of Drogheda? I'm quite sure the Drogheda Borough Council would provide us with an official letter of repentance and apology. (Signatures must include Frank Godfrey.) After all, in case you haven't heard, apologies are all the rage.

Go me.

Maria

The mayor of Drogheda at the time, Maria Campbell O'Brien, then contacted me and asked me if I would attend the reception for the English delegation. She wanted to present a united front. I hesitated at first. But of course, on reflection I was delira and excira to attend. Turned out that they didn't in fact have any letter of apology or support from Huntingdon Town Council and they had even less support from Prime Minister Blair. But sure, the craic was good. And I got some more PR mileage out of the entire incident for the heritage centre. Unfortunately, it wasn't enough and our naive foray into the heritage business was soon over. Turned out that being completely idealistic about a living and breathing business wasn't enough to keep it alive. Who knew?

Kevin's grandad Joe

A strange thing happened in early 2004 though, as I was innocently trying to swing the lead one day at work. I got a call from Kevin Stanley, an old footballing mate of mine.

'Tom, you write history books,' he said. Hmm. In a way. I suppose. That much I knew already. I needed more. 'Would you be interested in writing my grandfather's biography? He was involved in the Rising. The family have agreed that we will cut you in on the publishing deal. We have loads of documents.'

Well, if you know anything about writing books and getting them published, you'll know that I found this quite hilarious. So many things. Firstly, who in the name of Jaysus would be interested in some anonymous ex-Sunday League footballer's grandfather, unless his name was Collins or De Valera?! Oh, they have loads of documents? Well, that changes everything. 'Are you for feckin' real?' I wanted to say to Kevin. But since he was a mate, I didn't want to seem like a complete dick.

I was effusive. 'Erm,' I said hesitatingly.

'Tell you what,' said Kevin just a split second before I told him to shove his grandfather's cherished life story sideways up his arse and welcome him to the real world. 'Meet me and sure we can talk it through,' he said.

I immediately kicked for touch and agreed to see him. At worst it would be a chance to catch up and at best...there was no at best.

What the hell did I know about the Rising? Besides, I'm pretty sure his grandfather was a lovely man, but no publisher is going to publish his story. Especially if I write it. The Rising?! The very idea of writing anything about such an iconic time in Irish history frightened the crap out of me. I could almost hear Connolly and Pearse turning in their graves. Poor Kevin is going to get a landing when I tell him that I'm not really a historian and that when it comes to this stuff I can just about tell the difference between a rising and a falling.

Anyway, we met at the appointed hour. After we discussed the vicissitudes of his animalistic sliding tackles, and *just* as I was about to quash this poor man's book dreams, Kevin reached into a filing cabinet and pulled out a folder. Aw shit. Here we go. He then laid out some brownish-coloured sheets on the table. There was handwriting on them with bits scratched out in pen and notes along the side. 'These were all handwritten by Pearse in the GPO during Easter Week,' he said nonchalantly.

More documents. And these were written by Michael Collins. 'Oh and did you know that Collins was a great sprinter and long jumper?' asked Kevin, as I stared at the documents open-mouthed. 'Well, here's the results of the 100-yard dash and the long jump from Frongoch in Wales in the summer of 1916, both of which Collins won by a country mile.'

To explain the magnitude of what Kevin was showing me it's probably best that I fast forward slightly. Years later, in 2012, I'm driving aimlessly along, and I'm listening to the curator of the National Museum, Dr Pat Wallace, being interviewed on RTE Radio 1. When asked 'What is the most significant thing that was donated to the museum during your time there?' he had no hesitation in saying 'The Joe Stanley collection of documents'. And here was Kevin laying it all out on the table in front of me. Little old me.

Standing on the shoulders of giants

Suffice to say, I started to read all I could about the Rising. I travelled to Frongoch and stood on the hallowed ground where about 2,000 Irish men were incarcerated in a concentration camp following the Rising, and the hairs stood up on the back of my nads. It was eventually to become known as the University of Revolution.

I engaged with the Stanley family and got to know their grandfather very well, albeit posthumously. But that didn't prevent him and me from forming a unique connection. I wrote the book. I contacted Steve and he agreed to publish. *Joe Stanley: Printer to the Rising* was published by Brandon in 2005.

'Hey,' said Kevin at one stage during the proceedings, 'this is the perfect antidote to that Cromwell shite you're always banging on about.'

Oh yeah. Good point, Kevin.

Finally, a *historian* who actually agrees with me!

And so back to that Cromwell shite that I'm always banging on about. As the weeks, months and years passed I kept a close eye on the stuff that the real historians were saying. In many ways, it was just like my book had never been published. Most people of an academic persuasion simply ignored it. Then in 2007 a really odd thing happened. Philip McKeiver with an MA Hons in history – so definitely an academic – came out with a book he called *A New History of Cromwell's Irish Campaign*. I say it was odd, because he referenced my book quite a lot, seemed to want to discredit the logistics of the battle of Drogheda that I had espoused, and decided that he was now the one who had discovered that Cromwell didn't massacre civilians. I had no problem whatsoever with this and I contacted McKeiver at the time to tell him it was great that he had come to the same conclusion as I did. Isn't this great – a real historian came to the same conclusion as me! I think he was completely nonplussed, which was grand. Of course, McKeiver described me as an 'Irish historian', which was frustrating. He was clearly oblivious to the fact that I have a massive chip on my shoulder about that. My badge of honour. NOT a fricking historian. Get it?!

And just when things were going so well

But the diehards were having none of it. In an article entitled 'The Curse of Cromwell' in *History Ireland* in 2008, probably the foremost authority on Cromwell in Ireland, Prof. Micheál Ó Siochrú, took issue with my work when he wrote the following.

An honourable enemy?

One book relating specifically to the topic of Cromwell and Ireland, Tom Reilly's *Cromwell: An Honourable Enemy*, has proved particularly controversial. As the title suggests, Reilly approached the topic from the premise that Cromwell's brutal reputation in Ireland was entirely unjustified, the result, he argues, of a deliberate distortion of the facts by nationalist historians. It is an interesting if hardly original idea, but in his eagerness to prove this thesis Reilly simply dismissed or ignored contrary evidence. As C. H. Firth said of Thomas Carlyle's approach to Cromwell, 'like too many other historians he found in the past just what he went to the past to find'.

That was fair enough. The good professor was entitled to his opinion. But no sledgehammers or nuts. Hmm. There was a pattern that seemed to be emerging here. These historians were dismissing my work, but they *still* weren't really offering anything in response to my arguments. No forensic deconstructions of my text were forthcoming. Or at least, the arguments that they had raised didn't really cut the mustard. I figured that a dismissal was enough for them and anyway, how could I possibly be taken seriously? I was an amateur FFS. Not really worth the effort of taking head-on. This was the almost overwhelming conclusion of academia. Every historian who ever studied the period practically agreed. But of course, I had discovered Samuel Rawson Gardiner. I also discovered Thomas Carlyle, who was in agreement with Gardiner that Cromwell did not deliberately massacre civilians in Ireland. So, as Ó Siochrú patronisingly says, mine was 'hardly an original idea'.

Janey mac! A documentary on Cromwell in Ireland! I'm totally in. Where do I sign?

It was also around 2008 that I heard from a friend of a friend of a friend of a friend that there was going to be a documentary made about Cromwell in Ireland, called *Cromwell in Ireland*. The production was going to be made by Tile Films. And as soon as I heard this, I contacted the production company and asked them to involve me or my work in some way. I figured this was going to be a super opportunity to finally get the word out to the masses. Imagine. A brand-new documentary. Specifically about Cromwell and Ireland. The possibilities were endless. The big time beckoned. A book is one thing. But a documentary! Sure, with my fresh evidence they'll probably take hand and all. I sent an e-mail. Nothing. I sent another e-mail. Nothing. I called.

Nobody would talk to me. I sent another e-mail. Nada. Welcome to my life. Then I got word that Prof. Micheál Ó Siochrú was going to present the two-part series. Aw, shit. He's not exactly my biggest fan. No wonder they weren't engaging with me. I was clearly just a crank. A contrarian. A looper. And when you start to feel that way it's time to back off. So, I didn't. Back off. I was too pissed off to back off.

Through the friend of a friend of a friend of a friend, I managed to get my hands on some still images of the upcoming documentary. One of the illustrations depicted civilians being killed. Bingo! Bastards. What were they thinking? This stuff was ancient. This stuff was incendiary. Why would they continue to peddle the traditional auld shite here in 2008!

Okay, so I'm an idiot. So what?!

As I was writing a column for the *Drogheda Independent* at this time, I did a news piece using the stills to illustrate it, saying that the upcoming documentary was simply going to tell the same old story. I heard later that I caused some consternation among the documentary makers by doing this, but I didn't care because I was a rebel. *Drogheda Independent* readers just threw their collective eyes up to heaven and said there's that local loon again. I'm sure the people in Tile Films thought I was just a loose cannon with a bad attitude. You do realise that I'm not saying all the things I did along the way were right. You know that, right? I often reacted in a stupid, tawdry way, but the more opposition that came from the historians, the more cavalier and obstinate I became. I simply couldn't help it. In fact, if I had a little humility, I'd be the perfect man. But alas…

On 9 September 2008 the first part of the documentary was shown on RTE. The second part, a week later. Interestingly, Prof. Ó Siochrú also had a book coming out at the same time that he called *God's Executioner*, which was also to be about Ollie in Ireland. The bould Ollie was getting plenty of coverage at this time. I was extremely happy to see this of course, but I had not influenced the narrative in any way whatsoever. I had, of course, completely rewritten the controversial aspects of the entire period! So that was particularly frustrating. Well, another way of putting that is that I hadn't quite been found out yet. I watched Ó Siochrú deliver the narration. I watched him say the words that at Drogheda 'an indeterminate number of civilians were killed'. I wanted to slap him silly. Because he just added fuel to that nationalistic narrative. He said 'civilians'. He didn't say whether or not they were armed. He just fed the traditional beast. And now he was about to bring out a book. On Cromwell. In Ireland. Here comes the sledgehammer. I gotta protect my nuts!

Chapter 6

2008–2014

Money, money, money

But wait! Between the non-appearance of that serious challenge from the academics who didn't agree with me, young McKeiver's offering, and the plethora of positive reviews from ordinary humans I was getting on Amazon, my confidence was building. My self-absorption reached new levels. When I was having my spat with Frank he seemed intent on insisting that the historians didn't agree with me and that this was somehow an incontrovertible fact. But in my head, it didn't matter a jot that they didn't. Are we really saying that we need an actual expert to tell us what really happened at Drogheda and Wexford in 1649? Well, duh. I think we're big enough to be able to make up our own minds. And I, for one, certainly didn't need to be told.

And it wasn't long before the Holocaust was mentioned. 'So if you're denying Cromwell's massacres, you might as well say the Holocaust didn't happen,' came the cry from a rake of detractors on the Interweb. That was impressive logic, I thought to myself. People are pretty much all over the place if you ask me. I should've listened to my mother. 'Never get involved with people,' she'd say. The comparison with Hitler became an ever-present one. But my point was very specific. I wasn't saying anything about Cromwell sending us all to hell or to Connaught, or the people who were rounded up and sent to Barbados as slaves, or all the land he robbed from the Irish. I was simply saying that he didn't kill civilians deliberately and that was really a very small aspect of the Irish wars. Albeit a very significant one.

While I was making various appearances at local history society soirées all over the country, I decided at this point that

I would refuse to take any money for my trouble. This was because I kept being accused of being in it for the money. It didn't make any difference where I had to travel. Even if I had to stay overnight. I didn't want to be accused of being in this revision game for any gain whatsoever.

Mammy, the Coleman's here!

With all of this Cromwell stuff in the air around this time, on 21 September 2008 the *Sunday Independent* carried a review of *Honourable Enemy* by some dude called Marc Coleman. It kinda came completely out of the blue – although Steve did actually release the book again at this time, under the Brandon imprint but with a different cover, and this time in softback. So that was three iterations of the book to date. Flippin' eck! Coleman denounced it from the highest height and suggested it should simply be thrown into a rubbish tip. I considered legal action but apparently people have the right to their opinions when they're doing book reviews. Grrr. It was the most scathing rebuke yet, and there were plenty to choose from. The worst part about that particular edition of the *Sunday Independent* is that it was quite rough on the buttocks.

The experts have spoken.
Who would dare question the experts?

Around this time, I got an early look at Ó Siochrú's *God's Executioner* on its publication, because I was asked by *Ireland On Sunday* to review it. Okay, here goes. This was the first large volume of work from one of my major critics. Brace yourself, Reilly. Here it comes. I was finally going to be taken down. My wings were about to be clipped. And all sorts of other clichés of a similar nature. First thing I did was to check the index to see if my name was there. Not a sign. So, he hasn't mentioned me by name in the text. Grand. My book was, however, referenced in the bibliography. It was only years later when I got older and wiser that I realised there was no way he was ever going to mention me in his book. That would be tantamount to some acknowledgement of my work, so that definitely wasn't going to happen.

Interestingly, Ó Siochrú decided to use the contemporary newsbook *The Man in the Moon* as evidence to support the civilian massacre theory. He writes:

> *The Man in the Moon* picked up the allegations of civilian deaths the following week, claiming that the figure of 3,000 dead included 2,000 women and children.

He also writes:

> In early October *Mercurius Elencticus*, until then the most moderate of the news-sheets (at least in its Irish coverage), made a number of specific and shocking allegations. The dead at Drogheda included women and children.

So now we have two academics – and very significant academics of the modern era – using the words of *Mercurius Elencticus* and *The Man in the Moon*. When I was writing my books I had never come across either of these publications. And on the face of it, they were pretty damning to my thesis. Furthermore, Ó Siochrú also included the actual names of civilians who had died at Drogheda, so this also wasn't good.

> However, others, such as James Fleming, are described as 'murdered' while Henry Mortimer, an alderman of the town, was killed, 'being then about 70 years of age.'

Wow. It just shows ya. Here I was shooting my mouth off and he comes out with all this massacre-supporting stuff. Then, just for good measure, he writes:

The issue remains contentious to the present day, but the surviving evidence clearly shows that a significant number of non-combatants were killed during the storming of the town.

It really pissed me off that in his narrative MOS didn't differentiate between inhabitants that were armed from those that might not have been. For me, this just fans the flames of anti-British sentiment. And I have a problem with that. So, sue me.

The name's Reilly, Tom Reilly

I was shaken but I wasn't stirred. I wanted to challenge *Dr No*. After all, *You Only Live Twice*. The *Spectre* of MOS was beginning to loom large. I wanted solace. In fact I wanted a whole fricken *Quantum of Solace*. The cynic in me just wouldn't let it lie. I had far too much evidence in Cromwell's favour but my square pegs were not fitting into Ó Siochrú's round holes, if you'll forgive the expression. I simply had to do more research to check out the veracity of these revelations and so I got to work. By this time, there was a ginormous amount of research material online and I got deeper and deeper into the subject just by clicking my mouse at home. I didn't have to visit a library or an educational institution at all. This of course was always my *modus operandi*. Sure, I never went to any of these places. I visited the National Library once or twice but that was it really. I simply found all I needed in books and online.

Documentary, anyone?

Meanwhile, the world of TV documentaries had completely beguiled me. See, that's a whole new audience. Imagine viewers, not readers. I was determined to get this message to as many people as I could, so I began to contact documentary makers. Some of them were half interested in the story, companies like

Happy Endings and Bold Puppy, but I just didn't seem to be able to convince any of them to either invest or procure funding for a film. There were several more that I met with, but I just can't remember them now, and I didn't keep records. But you gotta trust me on this. It's an interesting story, but just not tellyrrific enough. Every now and again, maybe on a twice-yearly basis, I would send an e-mail to as many documentary makers as I could find online to see if I would get a bite. Sometimes I did and sometimes I didn't. But nothing ever came of it and I never got past the first meeting. Must have been my BO.

The growing chip on my shoulder

In general it bothered me that the academics seemed to be ignoring me, in the main. At least that's the way it felt. In reality, of course, many others actually agreed with me, as Jason attested to earlier in his anti-me diatribe. So, like the regular e-mail to documentary makers, I would send out an e-mail to seventeenth-century experts every now and again to see if they would like to produce a book of essays on this subject, but I never got any positive responses. At least, none that took the idea onto the next level. Some of them were lovely, don't get me wrong. The inimitable Prof. Ronald Hutton for instance became somewhat of a fan and always wished me well, even though he wouldn't get directly involved with any of my zany ideas. I often wondered what I was doing wrong. This history business is a tough business to be in when you're trying to change things.

History Today

In the summer of 2012, I approached Paul Lay, the then editor of the UK magazine *History Today*, to see if they would accept an article from me. They were delighted. Well, that's the way I read it. They might have reluctantly agreed with large doses of trepidation and the intention to tell me 'no thanks' when they actually saw what I wrote. Thankfully, that didn't happen. An article written by me, entitled 'Cromwell: The Irish Question', appeared in their September issue of that year. I was completely chuffed. Look at the heights I was scaling. Real history magazines publishing stuff that I wrote. On a complete roll, I approached Tommy Graham in *History Ireland* around the same time. This was Ireland, my home country. 'Hey Tommy, can I write an article for *History Ireland* about my take on Cromwell?'

'No,' said Tommy.

And that was the end of that. Oh well.

Brace yissaselves. Here comes book number three

With Ó Siochrú having 'taken his best shot', it wasn't long before I felt another book coming on. Was that really the best he could do? While I was the only one who was experiencing this ongoing battle with these historians in my head, namely Ó Siochrú, McElligott, Morrill, and Lenihan, their constant rebuffs were enough for me to keep my enthusiasm for the topic nicely boiling over.

Around this time I became engaged in an exchange of viewpoints by e-mail with a random Kerryman – someone I met online – over some weeks' duration. I'm not going to mention his name here, but you know who you are, Michael. He was extremely knowledgeable on the topic and he challenged my thesis quite significantly. I don't mind admitting that I had many weak moments along the way, and this was definitely one of them. But during the discourse I began to realise that it didn't really matter what I said to him – he was going to stick with the traditional version irrespective of the facts. This had obviously happened on numerous occasions over the years, but this guy was so tuned in, it made quite an impact on me. And so I decided that I probably had enough material here for another book. This is how *Cromwell Was Framed* was born.

I didn't have to go far looking for a controversial title. I had often harked back to the *Cambridge Evening News* article of 1999 that had the headline 'Irishman claims that Cromwell was Framed', and now was the perfect opportunity to use those three words in a meaningful sentence. It was in keeping with my controversial titles. I had also written a shit de-conversion book describing how I gave up religion that I called *Hollow Be Thy Name*, a line I clearly robbed from the satirical version of Our Lord's Prayer, or the Our Father in old money. I had wanted to call the book *Holy Shit*, but the publisher dissuaded me from going down that particular road. Here's the church, here's the steeple, look inside...yeah, not as popular as it used to be, is it? Anyway, what's that got to do with Cromwell, you might well ask. Yep. Not a damn thing.

A wee bit to do first

Anyway, I needed to deal with the information that was contained in *Mercurius Elencticus*, *The Man in the Moon* and these two Drogheda civilians that Ó Siochrú had mentioned by name, Mortimer and Fleming. They were irritating the shite out of me. Hey, maybe Fleming and Mortimer were just popping around to the shops in the middle of a slaughter and just forgot to put their armour on. What did I know?

And of course, the evidence of Thomas à Wood was constantly niggling at me. I also had to deal comprehensively with the words 'and many inhabitants' that seemed to be appended to a letter that Cromwell wrote to parliament after the siege of Drogheda. This was pretty damning, since on the face of it, Cromwell was admitting that he killed inhabitants. Okay, so he didn't say if they were armed, or unarmed. But hey ho. Maybe I had gotten this wrong, despite my own protestations. As far as I knew, Wood was, after all, a Cromwellian soldier who was actually in Drogheda at the time. And we know Cromwell was there too. That much is pretty certain.

A lot of people were flabbergasted that I preferred the word of Cromwell over all the other contrary evidence. When you consider that the Kremlin lie through their teeth about absolutely everything and anything and it doesn't even have to be during a war, how could I possibly believe Cromwell when he said that he didn't kill civilians? Well, it was mainly because I studied the man exhaustively and I simply don't believe he was a liar, in any aspect of his life. He was no Putin. And just for the record he was no Hitler. And I'm happy to confirm that most historians who have studied the man are of exactly the same opinion, including John Morrill. He may have been deluded in many things, but Cromwell was no liar. *Capisce?* He was often frank, brutally frank, and even when he wasn't frank, he probably looked frank. In my experience, when there are two versions of a story, the usual trend is that people will believe the version in which other people appear at their worst.

Ollie's letter and the 'and many inhabitants' conundrum

So, Cromwell's letter to parliament is a really good place to start. I discovered a wonderful online facility where you could access contemporary documents online. I wasn't supposed to be able to access them because I wasn't a member of an academic institution, but I managed to get past that by having a bit of craic with one of the gatekeepers – and I was in. In this business it's a well-known fact that Cromwell's original letter from Drogheda does not exist. The text is printed in a leaflet or pamphlet that was produced by parliament as a way of bringing the news from Ireland to the English people.

In the book *Honourable Enemy*, I had relied on Thomas Carlyle's nineteenth-century assertion that the words 'and many inhabitants' were added by the printer of the pamphlet, a bloke called John Field, and I got into a whole lot of trouble for saying that. Jason, who was a complete expert on printing in the seventeenth century, was aghast that I would suggest such a thing, even though I was just quoting Carlyle. Loads of other people also pointed out the flaws in my argument.

'So how come John Field wasn't punished for saying such a thing?' they cried. If inhabitants were killed, are we really saying that the printer simply added the words and didn't get to pay for it later. Such a huge transgression. Carlyle had said that there was no sign of those three words in the old pamphlets. But now I had access to those old pamphlets. So I can just get stuck into them and read them all word for word.

Looking through these news-sheets – the actual newspapers of the day – I discovered several things that seemed to make sense. First of all, I found a contemporary reference to the fact that some of the civilians of Drogheda were actually armed. Boom! So now, any reference whatsoever to inhabitants could easily mean that they were armed inhabitants. This was not unusual of course, just in case you think it was. In the same way that all over England people were taking up arms to defend their towns and cities in the civil war there, the exact same thing happened in Ireland. Drogheda was full of people who were no doubt on each side of the divide. In fact, one of the things that we actually do know is that there was a civilian plot to try to get the military occupants to allow Cromwell access to the town so he could simply take it over without a shot being fired. Put that in your smoke and pipe it. I also discovered proof that Lord Ormond – who was Cromwell's chief adversary in Ireland and leader of the royalist coalition – had ordered all superfluous people out of Drogheda so the soldiers could be fed. He didn't want to have to feed civilians, so he told them to sling their hook. Get out of town. True story.

To make a long story boring, I soon discovered that there were seven news-sheets that printed the list of those 'slain at Drogheda'. Turns out that only two of them had the three offending words included. Furthermore, reading through the documents and the work of academic writers who evaluated them, it was clear to me that the official government pamphlet was actually printed in a bit of a hurry. It was also obvious that the list was simply added to the end of the letter because there was some space left in the 16-page pamphlet on the page where the actual letter ended. Having a printing background, I realised that sheets are printed in multiples of four. This was a 16-page pamphlet. And since there was a left-over space on one of the pages, the printers more than likely inserted the list of those slain at the end of Cromwell's letter with a clear demarcation line – and for centuries Cromwell himself would be accused of admitting to massacring civilians simply because of this innocuous printing procedure. The point would be, of course, that somebody wrote the words 'and many inhabitants', but the counterpoint would clearly be – that they were armed and involved in the conflict. And I had found the evidence for this. This was the only thing that would fit with all of the other evidence. So now I had a new spin on these three offending words. And this was all going into my new book. The protestations of McElligott, Ó Siochrú and Morrill were all looking decidedly weaker now. Okay, I know all this is potentially boring history stuff, but it was such a revelation to me and I was so excited by these discoveries. I knew I was right. I just simply had to work it all out.

So that was Cromwell's letter sorted. But even worse (for them) was to come.

Fleetwood Wood, Wood Fleetwood

Wood was one of the other things I had to figure out. Jason had gone into print using Wood's evidence to refute mine. Ó Siochrú also used it to support the civilian massacre theory. I simply couldn't believe what I discovered. Me?! The answer was literally there on the Internet. Millions of academics had completely missed this. I wondered how much I could find. One of the problems was that I might easily struggle with interpreting this document because it seemed all over the place. Who was who? What was what? Without any historical training,

I could easily get something wrong. But that didn't really faze me, so I just ploughed on to see where I'd get, like I had always done.

So, everybody knows that Thomas à Wood's account of killing virgins and holding children up as human shields is a contemporary piece of evidence from an eyewitness that comes from a book that was written by his brother Anthony à Wood. Simples. It's actually given away in the title of the book, *The Life of Anthony à Wood, written by himself.* WRONG! On every count. This book was not written by Anthony à Wood. It was cobbled together by several people one hundred and twenty-three years after the events at Drogheda and it could easily have been interfered with by any of them. And this was supposed to be the only eyewitness who gives us details of civilian deaths at Drogheda. Do me an effen favour. Wood's account is a complete load of bullshit. As the years passed, more stuff would emerge about Wood, but this is where I was at this point in the story. As far as I was concerned at this time, no court in any land at any time in history would convict Cromwell of killing civilians based on this complete crap. But the maddest thing about this was that I was the one who found this out. Using a few clicks of the mouse. Little old *me*? Now I was really on a serious roll. (I Wood discover more about Wood later in my research, but that's all you're getting for now. This is in chronological order, remember?) All I had to do now was work on *Mercurius Elencticus* and *The Man in the Moon* and I was good to go.

But this was going to be a real challenge. How could I possibly argue with newspapers that came out in the weeks following the siege of Drogheda? These were surely sacrosanct. After all, Jason was a huge advocate of the words that these newspapers carried. And we've seen what Ó Siochrú said about them. I needed to find something really good if I was to dismiss this stuff. In fact, all of the other evidence could go and take a run and jump if these two newspapers were accurate.

The two men who actually framed Cromwell

So, what do we know about the people who actually wrote the articles in the papers? Reporters of the day, like. And how are we going to find out? Surely this was far too long ago, and we wouldn't have any information about them at all. They were bound to be pretty obscure individuals. Well, if you were thinking that then you'd be completely wrong. And how do I know this? Because Jason McElligott (among others) worked it all out for us. In his research Jason found out that the writers of these news-sheets were complete loopers who were totally anti-parliament, complete propagandists and would write whatever the hell they wanted to because paper would never refuse ink. He derided them up the wazoo, did our Jason. And the hilarious thing? Jason himself was using this 'evidence' to support his own interpretations. I mean, c'mon. What exactly are we saying there? Something's not right in the State of Deutschmark. He completely discredits George Wharton (the writer of *Mercurius Elencticus*) and John Crouch (the writer of *The Man in the Moon*) and then proceeds to use their shite as arguments for a civilian massacre. I was gobsmacked. Historians, eh? Janey mac. Seems like they can just say what they like and people just believe them because they're historians. Well, you have your shite. I was elated that I had managed to rebuff the rebuffs of the historians – and then some.

Citations, anyone? Nah. Thanks anyway

So now I was ready to publish the book. And I was obviously going to call it *Cromwell Was Framed*. But there was the relatively small matter of actually getting a book deal. Oh yeah. Here we go again. Back into the lions' den. It was heartbreaking. Here I was with something I thought was important and would copper-fasten my place in the world of history because I was exposing the subjective opinions of these historians and any other historian for that matter. I had come a long way from writing an article for the Old Drogheda Society. Anyway, after several more rejection letters, I eventually found John Hunt Publishing in the UK. They agreed to publish under their imprint Chronos Books. Mine was the first book to come out under that particular imprint.

During its compilation I was completely determined that this was not to be an academic publication. I had very strong reasons for this, however flawed they were. And believe me, many people thought this was crazy. There was just no way I was going to try and include citations or references of any sort in this book. I was castigated by so many people for not knowing what I was doing with the first book. I still hadn't done any history training, so I still hadn't a clue how this worked. Instead, I thought I would include images of the actual contemporary documents and let people read them for themselves.

Here we go again with the shit reviews

Cromwell Was Framed was published in 2014 and there was a minor flurry of publicity surrounding it. Probably the most auspicious publication that paid any attention to it was the *Irish Times*. They had a real historian actually review it. Now I don't know about you, but I would have thought there was an absolute heap of historians out there ready, willing and able to review books. There was no way they were going to get one of the four of my primary detractors to review it. Could they? Yep. You guessed it. Pádraig Lenihan reviewed it. Aw jeez. This can't be good. But I've made an incredible case. Have I not made an incredible case? The whole book was intended to expose these historians and make my point.

Here are some of Lenihan's words:

This is an angry little book. Tom Reilly lambastes three academics – John Morrill of Cambridge, Micheál Ó Siochrú of Trinity College Dublin and Jason McElligott of Marsh's Library – because they panned his *Cromwell: An Honourable Enemy* (1999) out of 'vested historical interests'. *Cromwell Was Framed* sets out an apparently more nuanced version of Reilly's original assertion: large numbers of innocent civilians were not deliberately killed at the storming of Drogheda and Wexford in 1649.

Reilly's style is accessible and lively, but hero worship rather skews historical judgment, specifically in his choice of what evidence to accept and how to interpret that evidence.

Reilly fully accepts only eyewitness accounts of what happened at Drogheda and Wexford published shortly after the events they describe. This blanket ban privileges accounts emanating from the winners, as competing narratives took longer and more circuitous routes into print. Reilly boasts, for example, that in *Cromwell: An Honourable Enemy* he already demolished a shockingly graphic account by a perpetrator of how he and his comrades killed women and children at St Peter's Church in Drogheda.

In fact, Reilly's critique betrayed an inadequate grasp of contemporary idiom and context. A 'most handsome virgin' was 'arrayed in costly and gorgeous apparel', the perpetrator said. How, scoffed Reilly, could the soldier tell she was a virgin? Was it not ridiculous to suppose she would dress up and carry jewels in such dire circumstances? (The author can get it badly wrong when he tries to set a context. To take just one example: the 'entire Pale community' did not face off against the native Irish in the 1641 rising. Had the Palesmen done so, the insurrection would have been a short-lived affair.) Reilly now relies essentially on the grounds that the confession did not find its way into print for over a century and the perpetrator's brother, who wrote the account, may have been a closet Catholic.

Frankly, I don't get it. I think there's more going on here than meets the eye. I think some of these guys are embarrassed that I exposed them. They've taken this too far now and it's impossible for them to agree with me under any circumstances. There may also be nationalistic tendencies behind some of this, but at this stage I was beginning to think that it was more the fact that they couldn't accept I was right. Now, I know others came before me (like Carlyle and Gardiner) – and hopefully more will come after me – but there is no question that I lead the charge of Cromwell apologists when it comes to Ireland these days. Google it.

Maybe it's my pugnacity that irks them. I dunno. But again, Lenihan offered nothing of any substance as an argument except to repeat the evidence of Thomas à Wood in the most wishy-washy way. And as for his point that I was relying on 'accounts of what happened at Drogheda and Wexford published shortly after the events' – without screaming this in capitals – OF COURSE I EFFING WAS! Don't go telling me that post-Restoration (dating from 1660 and beyond) stuff is as important as primary source evidence (dating from 1649). Sheesh. I actually despair right now. Is that what he's really saying? The whole point of *Cromwell Was Framed* was to offer the evidence in chronological order, as it appeared, by the week, the month and then the year to see what stacks up. And one of the main things I discovered was that – without the *Mercurius Elencticus* and *The Man in the Moon* claptrap from Wharton and Crouch respectively – there was absolutely no suggestion from anyone in the universe that Cromwell killed civilians at either Drogheda or Wexford for 11 years. Eleven shitting years! It was only when Cromwell's republic failed, and the Restoration of the monarchy happened, that it became open season on all things Cromwellian and people could write what they wanted in a time when it was perfectly acceptable just to lie about everything if it made your enemies look bad. Actually, that's more or less the way wars always have been throughout history – I get that. But to understand how the Interregnum (the time between monarchs) was excoriated (I love that word) by Charles II's Restoration crew both in Ireland and in England is to fully appreciate prexactly what these seventeenth-century spin doctors were capable of.

Annoying the locals again

The book didn't go down that well among some locals either. I don't know if it's anything to do with living in a border county, but a bloke called Mici Mac Ruairi wasn't at all happy with me. Using the pages of the *Drogheda Independent* on 26 February 2014, Mici wrote:

> Dear Sir,
>
> Is this Tom Reilly lad for real? I think he is living in his own little bubble. Oliver Cromwell was like Hitler, Stalin, William of Orange, Longshanks and Maggie Thatcher. He was the devil. Seriously – how can you say that Cromwell was innocent? You should stop while you're ahead, you are making a show of yourself. The next thing you'll be telling me is that Scarlet Street did not get its name from the blood of the innocent victims slaughtered by Cromwell.

Aw, feck. I dunno how to break this to you, Mici – but the Scarleh Streeh ting is just a myt.

A few months passed and Mici went for me again. This time on 20 August of that year. Writing to the same local paper Mici said:

> You know the evenings are getting darker when you see Tom Reilly, the saviour of Cromwell, coming out of his

cave. I don't know what planet he's on but he's a disgrace to Drogheda, to the county of Louth and to the country of Ireland.

There's no answer to that really. Good job I have tik skin.

Imagine for a moment if I had declared that the 1916 Rising leaders had never been executed; that the Great Famine had never taken place; or that the *Titanic* wasn't built in Belfast. The world would rightly disagree and would point to a plethora of evidence to prove their points. The arguments would have ended before gaining any traction. To me, this is the exact same situation. So far, no solid evidence has ever been produced by any historian anywhere that would support their 'disagreement' with my contentions.

Not exactly a bestseller but am working on it

Well, my work is done here. I've finally told the world the real deal about Cromwell in Ireland. Twice now, in fact. And I've rebuffed the academic rebuffers with real evidence. I am clearly some sort of genius. I can hang my pugnacity up in a framed picture on the wall and move on with my life. Story over. However, there was one small problem. In 2014 the world's population was 7.254 billion. The Irish diaspora all over the world is estimated at about 80 million. At the time of writing (here in 2023), *Cromwell Was Framed* has sold just under 1,000 copies. The John Hunt Publishing process gives me very accurate information. And that took eight years. Eight Jaysus years, and I still haven't sold 1,000 effen copies. Yep, I'm in this for the money all right. In fact, when I did the book deal with John Hunt Publishing, I told them to give all my royalties to charity, so I could say that I was giving all my royalties to charity. I'd say that charity is fairly pissed off now. Duz no money in books. Well, not the ones I write. My advice to aspiring writers – marry money.

Chapter 7

2014–2022

The sunny south-east and other stories

So far, I'm sure you've noticed that most of my focus has been on Drogheda. There isn't much Wexfordy stuff going on really. I don't have any problem with the people of Wexford, you understand. Bastards. Only joking. See, it's funny. But by virtue of the numbers of the dead soldiers alone, Drogheda gets top billing in this show. The biggest blot on Ollie's career, as they say in all the best history books. The fact remains that while Wood is credited with being the 'only eyewitness' who gives us details of civilian killings at Drogheda, there is nobody at all who gives us details for deliberate civilian killings at Wexford. Accidental, yes. Deliberate, no. I know you're probably asking yourself, how on earth did this massacre bullshit gain so much traction? Or not. Could depend on your politics, I suppose. But if you're being objective, at the very least you have to admit that there's reasonable doubt. With no eyewitness detail of the Wexford events, I could of course just leave it there and not analyse any more evidence, I suppose.

What about the petition of the people of Wexford, I hear you all ask? Well, if you don't know, here's the thing: When Charles II's arse was back on the throne the dislocated people of Wexford decided to petition him for the restoration of their properties. As I said, I don't get involved in judging the land-grabbing skulduggery of these times. To me, it's history and very little else. The prevailing religious, political, military and economic circumcisions prevailing at the time are all things that it's literally impossible to get your head around these days. Might as well have been a different planet. Those bastard Brits came over and stole our land no matter what way you dress it up. And when they took Wexford, they fecked all the locals who had taken the side of the king in the war – which most if not all of them did – off their properties and kept it for themselves.

The petition itself still exists. There are actual images of it available online, if you look hard enough. There are plenty of historians who will point to this document as proof that 1,500 innocent civilians were massacred at Wexford. But there is a fundamental problem with the petition of the people of Wexford. Naturally. What else would you expect *me* to say?! Sometimes I feel like an old man (can somebody get me one please?!) who's clinging on against immense odds to some ancient convention that has no place in the third millennium. But there's just no way this petition works, and here at the Bureau of Misplaced Optimism it was my intention to discredit this 'evidence' as completely untrustworthy.

Cromwell's sacking of Wexford is almost always treated the same as that of Drogheda. In *God's Executioner*, Micheál Ó Siochrú fails to make any distinction between both sets of demographics, military and civilian. Most significantly, he fails to point out that there is very solid evidence to suggest that many of the Wexford townsmen took up arms in defence of their town. This is a hugely important point when it comes to the reports of the battle being written because there are contemporary accounts that mention the deaths of 'inhabitants' or 'townsmen'. Clearly, local men in arms are not innocent civilians. But like many before him, Ó Siochrú does not make the distinction between local townsmen in arms and non-military members of the local community, especially women and children. Indeed, he writes:

Cromwell wrote that over 2,000 Irish soldiers and civilians, including Sinnott, died, as the English 'put to the sword all that came their way.' According to a petition of the surviving inhabitants, all the men, women and children of the town 'to a very few' were killed during the assault, while a clerical account described how 'the blood lust of the soldiers flooded the streets and houses'...The deaths of large numbers of civilians at the hands of soldiers under his command further tarnished Cromwell's reputation with the Catholic Irish.

Ó Siochrú clearly wants the world to think that women and children were indiscriminately massacred by Cromwell's troops at Wexford. Furthermore, he has no reservations about using non-primary source, post-Restoration evidence to suggest that the vast majority of the women and children of Wexford were slaughtered in cold blood, when there is not one contemporary eyewitness account to support this. Maybe Ó Siochrú is correct to cite this source in the context that he does. Maybe the petition of the people of Wexford to Charles II is historically correct and all of the popular eyewitness source accounts (including the accounts reported in newsbooks) from those who were there on the day are suspect. But if we are to accept the words of the petitioners, then we must also accept what they say about Drogheda:

Oliver Cromwell arriveing with a powerful army in Ireland in the year 1649 and having upon the taking of Drogheda put all the inhabitants and soldiers to the sword that the example thereof might strike terror into the hearts of the inhabitants of other townes.

We already know this not to be true, in as far as we can be sure about anything from this period of history. All of the inhabitants of Drogheda killed, as well as the garrison, is quite a claim. This allegation goes some way to explaining just how far the petitioners would go in order to try to regain their properties. This petition was an effort to both curry favour with Charles II as soon as his royal seat had warmed the English throne again and encourage him to restore the Catholics of Wexford to their properties. Sweeping post-Restoration statements from disgruntled parties with a clear vested interest is a poor example of evidence to support the innocent civilian atrocity theory. The petition of the people of Wexford is clearly at odds with the surviving contemporary evidence.

But what of the non-aggressive civilian community of Wexford: old men and old women, the cobblers, the innkeepers, the merchants, their wives, their children and babies? On 9 October Ormond had ordered Sinnott to evacuate the 'unnecessary people such as old men, women and children' from the town. This is *huge*. Again with all the mouths to feed. He did the exact same thing at Drogheda, remember? We had this already!

The Wexford wimmin who were crap at swimmin'

Since the attack took place on the 11th, the governor had two days to send whatever remaining civilians there were from the town. However, we know from a contemporary report that some women, at least, didn't make it. As the town was being stormed it seems that some members of the garrison boarded boats alongside a number of women and the boats sank as they made their way across the estuary. It is worth noting that when it comes down to the detail, there is just one eyewitness account that mentions these deaths of women, and it is equally worth noting that these deaths are not reported as being deliberate, but as the result of an unfortunate set of circumstances. The poor things.

Come and have a go if you think you're clever enough

Anyway, where was I? Back to the story. Oh yeah, taking all of the evidence into account, I was completely convinced that certain historians were looking at this very peculiarly indeed. What exactly is going on? I'm an idiot and *I* get it. It was nice to see positive reviews on Amazon for *Cromwell Was Framed* and I could see that I was beginning to change some people's minds. But it became apparent very quickly that selling 1,000 books wasn't going to make the impact on humanity about Cromwell that I had hoped at the outset. So, what to do.

As the months went by and the book took on a life of its own, it was also nice to see that the historians who I had defended myself against had crawled back under the rock from which they had first emerged. No more challenges were forthcoming. They simply got on with the business of teaching impressionable minds anti-English hogwash. Of course in their world I wasn't even a cursory thought. But in mine, I was just waiting and waiting for one of them to take that sledgehammer out and crack my nuts. C'mon! Take your best shot, yis bastards! Put me back in my box. Shut me up. How could I be right and you be wrong? You guys are the fricken experts!

Kissing and making up with Historian A

It was also around this time that Historian A and I made up, no doubt you'll be disappointed to hear. There's no point in leaving our spat hanging out there if there was a genuine coming together, which really did happen. Without yet revealing his/her/its identity, I was happy that we could both find closure, even if I was the only one really looking for it. As a real bona fide historian he works in the business and actually teaches students about this stuff. Well, Ireland is a small country, and we soon developed a mutual acquaintance. When I started banging on and on at the mutual acquaintance about how Historian A had destroyed my confidence back in the early days, it seemed that this was getting back to Historian A. Anyway, the natural thing to do now was to try to patch things up.

As part of the patching-up process, Historian A – and fair play to his fiddler's elbow – invited me into his educational institution to speak to his students, which I duly did. Following the session, he and I sat down in his office, and we ironed out the past. I was delighted. I don't hold grudges and it turned out that he doesn't either. Of course, the only meeting of minds that day concerned the public barney we had; there was no way in hell that he was ever gonna agree with me on this particular subject. Nor I with him. But we moved on and that was progress indeed.

Simon says

When in 2015 the producers of the documentary *Simon Reeve's Ireland* met to discuss their upcoming programme on the culture, history and beliefs of people on the island of Ireland, somebody must have suggested that there was a lone Irishman – from Drogheda no less – trenchantly defending Oliver Cromwell's genocidal reputation in that town. This was quirky. This was unusual. Probably some local eccentric. Perfect for TV. If you haven't guessed already – this was me.

The producers' interest is indicative of the gradual shift in the perception of Cromwell's military campaign in Ireland that has taken place over the last 20 years or so. Like the chronological stages of grief, the various phases in this long process of a country coming to terms with the death of a precious tradition may take tens of years. Essentially, we are still at stage one: denial. But Reeve's interest in the topic indicated that the tide certainly has the potential to turn. Although right now, it's just a teeny-weeny ripple.

Ireland is no longer the place it was in the sixties of my childhood. Church and State no longer have the iron grip on the population that they once had. Historically, of course, more people have died of religion than of cancer. I'm an atheist now anyway, thang God. While Reeve's inclusion of this subject in his programme signifies a possible stage of general 'bemusement', a general reluctance to revise our understanding of the period clearly proves that 'acceptance' may be a significant number of years away yet. But it *is* inevitable. Delineating between 'civilian' and 'combatant' is probably the most important aspect of this issue, and the accepted massacre story doesn't attempt to do this in any way because it doesn't suit Ireland's 'victim of the English' narrative.

But as the time passed, no serious rebuff came from any of the academics. Not one. My arguments were still intact. And I was checking. Trust me. Any publication that came out about Cromwell, I was first in the queue to get it. It still seemed that in general the world of academia was just ignoring me. And the problem with me is that I really don't like being ignored. What the hell was the problem anyway? So, Cromwell wasn't such a bollix after all. Jeez. It's like 400 years ago FFS! Is it something to do with the fact that I'm not an academic and I have literally taught my granny to suck eggs here?

Time to swing into action again. Between the hops and the trots, the rigs and the jeels, I had managed to acquire the e-mail addresses of several academics over the years. And those I didn't have, it was easy enough to get them by going on their respective university's website.

New idea for a book – wait till yis see this!

I decided to contact early modern experts to see if they would be interested in producing a book with a collection of essays on Cromwell in Ireland. I carefully selected the first batch of likely candidates, sent out a superlative e-mail that they simply would never be able to resist under any circumstances, and waited. Nothing. Nada. Zilch. Not one response. Undaunted (it takes a lot to daunt me), I chose another set of experts, sprinkled some glitter over my original splendiferous e-mail, and waited. This time, in my head I would probably have to tell them to form an orderly queue and I'd get back to them if I felt like it. Much like they were doing to me. I'm building this up so you can be thinking that nothing happened. But this time was different. I got a bite!

Young Professor Martyn Bennett from Nottingham Trent University replied and said that the idea sounded interesting. Jesus. No way? Okay, okay, so he was in. What the feck do I do now? I had one bite. It was enough! So I hopped on the next plane to Stansted, hired a car and drove straight to Oliver Cromwell's House in Ely. What better place to meet with my new partner in crime. Over lunch in a nearby pub we agreed to make a call for papers and see what we would get. I was beside myself with excitement. This guy was even treating me as some sort of equal. Okay, it wasn't a real comparison, and I would never pretend that it was, but he showed me so much respect! It was such a breath of fresh air. See, I had gotten so used to being dismissed or ignored throughout the years by historians of all shapes and sizes, it was simply a difficult thing to embrace – respect from an early modern historian. We got on like a house on fire and we parted with the task to get about ten other papers and then from this we would cobble a bit of an auld book together. Y'know. Give it a bit of an auld go.

Now we're sucking diesel

Now in my approach to other academics I could tell them that I had the esteemed Martyn Bennett on board, and they literally fell into my lap. The next one up was Pádraig Lenihan. Holy crap. Can you believe it? Sure, he and I didn't agree on stuff, but what the heck did that matter? He was gonna do an article for my, sorry our, new book. With Lenihan now on the team, along came Alan Marshall, John Cunningham, Eamon Darcy, David Farr, Nick Poyntz, Sarah Covington, James Scott Wheeler and Heidi Coburn. To you, they may all just sound like vowels and consonants thrown together to form sounds, like names, but to me, they were my peeps. Some of them were household names in the early modern business. And it was lil ole me who had convinced them to come on board. Well, Martyn convinced David Farr, but all of the others were down to me! Of course I was forgetting one little thing. We didn't have a publisher. Oh shit. Yeah, that could be tricky.

But having managed to convince a couple of publishers in the past that they really needed to invest money in my work, I figured this was gonna be a cinch. When they heard who my fellow contributors were, they would be bating down my door. Okay, that's not exactly what happened but suffice to say my approach to Liverpool University Press was successful. They offered us a contract and I was made up, as they say in Liverpool. The omens were good: my mother was born in Liverpool, I have loads of relations in Liverpool and I was a big Liverpool supporter, so the synergy seemed to be working on several levels.

Pretending to be a historian

As an amateur, and a kind of a chancer still really, I was determined that my name could not be attached to the book in any sort of editorial role, despite it being my brainchild. I was no more qualified to edit this than Rory McElroy was to represent Botswana in the Olympics, so I took on the role of Project Manager. I liaised with all of the contributors at every stage, and I collected all of the papers. I also inveigled two other luminaries, Professors Ray Gillespie and R. Scott Spurlock, to help with the editing chores. Effectively, I was the glue that put the thing together. This seems like another good time to mention that I failed history at school, and I never went to college. Look at me now, Ma!

There was one wobbly moment when the entire manuscript was submitted to the publisher that I must tell yis about. They sent the essays out to get peer reviewed. It's a thing. It seems that there are peers all over the country who like to review stuff, and this book was no exception. Well, speaking of 'exception', one of the peers reported back that everything was great except that the paper from Tom Reilly needed to be discarded. Fair play to Martyn, he jumped to my defence and we got over that particular hurdle, but it was gutch and toe for a while there. I actually considered letting the boat sail without me, but then I had a moment of clarity. This was MY ifeckindea! Soon, common sense prevailed, and the book was back in production, after I made several changes to my essay. I had to tone it down a little for the academic audience. Essentially, I just attacked the historians who had dismissed my work without properly contesting it with contrary evidence. I was pretty emboldened at this stage, and while I still thought something might be revealed that nobody had ever seen before, I was pretty happy that my case in Cromwell's favour was completely fireproof. To appreciate my confidence in this matter, it might be interesting to read my final paragraph. Thankfully, you don't have to buy the book, because I can repeat it here for your convenience.

Here it is in all its controversial glory:

Were large numbers of innocent civilians deliberately massacred? Did Cromwell do it, or did he not? Should we still be teaching children that Cromwell indiscriminately slaughtered entire town populations? Purveyors of Irish history will need to embrace this idea because inevitably the narrative outlined here will begin to emerge as the years pass. Those who don't will be left behind to become part of some insular, embittered partisan clique whose roots are planted firmly in obduracy. Experts can be fallible. So long as people flatter themselves that they must listen to experts simply because they are experts, so long as they are content to swallow the dicta of an authority with closed eyes, so long will history be a delusion and a snare.

Shit that's good. Isn't that good? BOOM! That'll put the cat among the pigeons.

The book was called *Cromwell and Ireland: New Perspectives*. That was Martyn's idea. I had no problem whatsoever with it. He could have called it *Goblin-Proofing One's Chicken Coop in Seventeenth-Century Pucklechurch* for all I cared. Anyway, since I had managed to assemble such an illustrious bunch of academics to contribute, I thought I'd really push the boat out – and I contacted Prof. Micheál Ó Siochrú to see if he would do a paper for the book. The good professor politely declined. I didn't take no for an answer, and I asked him to reconsider. Again, he politely declined. For a long time I was pretty disappointed that I couldn't manage to attract the leading Cromwell historian in Ireland to contribute, but after that agonising two minutes eventually passed, I managed to get over it.

I had hoped that the majority of contributors would embrace the notion of a rehabilitated Cromwell and that this book would now act as a catalyst for a change in perceptions. *This will be my legacy.* You're welcome, world. And while some of them did, notably my colleagues Martyn Bennett, James Scott Wheeler and John Cunningham, others avoided the controversy, which I was disappointed with. But hey ho. In anticipation I wrote a blurb that didn't make it to the book's cover, but at least now it will get some sort of an airing:

In Ireland a timeworn bitterness still simmers over the punitive 'Cromwellian' policies, for which Oliver Cromwell is largely held personally responsible as Lord Protector during the 1650s. It is Cromwell's name that history has attached to the settlement of Ireland by the English parliament. He himself has been explicitly accused of war crimes at the sieges of Drogheda and Wexford in 1649. New research now attempts to extricate the word 'Cromwell' from the 'Cromwellian' settlement. Led by Prof. Martyn Bennett, a team of period experts re-examine the military campaign with a long overdue shift of focus to other parliamentarian leaders. Included are reassessments of the backdrop and context of both the prevailing siege warfare strategy and Cromwell's controversial legacy throughout Ireland ever since. Fresh insights are offered concerning some of the major players including Ormond, Ireton, Broghill and Jones. The facts are skilfully marshalled throughout, presented impartially, and it is difficult not to conclude that Cromwell's roles in both the alleged atrocities of the military campaign and the implementation of the Irish land settlement have to date been greatly overstated. Often labelled as one of history's greatest enigmas, it is clear that Oliver Cromwell retains the ability to absorb us still. It remains to be seen if the more passive Cromwell that emerges here will in any way assuage the vile caricature of the man that Irish history, tradition and folklore have all long-since accepted.

I wasn't a million miles away with this description, but maybe it was too inflammatory or indeed not quite representative of the essays themselves to end up on the book. Suffice to say, a more passive Cromwell definitely did emerge. But I had long embraced the idea that it would take decades to unravel the bullshit that surrounds this period. And that this book is just another one of my contributions to society in my attempt to right this wrong. Okay, my name does not appear on the front cover, but those whose names do, know the level of my involvement. I'm not trying to say I'm great when I say that by the way. I'm trying to say that I'm completely amazing. How are you not getting that?

And the scores are in… Oh, no, not him again!

When the book came out, I contacted Tommy Graham, the editor of *History Ireland*, hoping that they might review the book. Tommy had no trouble agreeing to this and he kindly let me know that the review would appear in the September 2020 issue. I've had some bad reviews in the past, but that was definitely because it was all down to me. This time was different. This time I had a team of experts. And in my experience, experts tended not to speak negatively about other experts. They can certainly speak negatively about me – it's always open season on me – but since there were far more experts behind this book, the review was bound to be a good one.

The magazine came out. The review was by Professor Micheál Ó Siochrú. Aw, bugger!

So much for peer deference. It was a bad review. I felt sorry for the guys because I felt that MOS's opinions of my work had castigated them by association. He singled me out for special negative attention in the review, which was fine. Then I thought about it a bit more and I realised that they probably couldn't have given a fiddler's. Of course, me being me, I shot a letter off to the editor challenging the reviewer to provide the evidence for significant numbers of civilian deaths. The letter was published. At least Tommy Graham gave me the right to reply, which was really nice.

Tile Films again

The next interesting thing to happen around this time was my encounter with the documentary makers Tile Films. If you remember from my earlier rantings, Tile Films were the company who produced *Cromwell in Ireland*, who I contacted at that time and probably pissed them off royally. Well, in the day job, where I manage Ardgillan Castle in North County Dublin, we often get requests for filming from all and sundry in the film and TV business. Anyway, one day it was extremely busy in the place, and I was awoken from a deep slumber by this dude called Colin Farrell. No, not that dude, I said this dude. A different Colin Farrell. Well, we got talking, as you do, mainly because I like to befriend documentary makers just on the off chance that they might see some merit to doing a doc with me about this Cromwell shite.

It didn't take me long to realise that Colin was from Tile Films. Well, that was mainly because I knew they were coming some weeks before I met Colin, from e-mails that he had sent me, but that doesn't matter. Point is – now they would see the real cut of my jib. Colin, his brother Keith and his dad Dave Farrell were behind the Cromwell doc *Cromwell in Ireland* and it wasn't long before I began to win them over. Or maybe it was long. I can't really remember to be honest. Problem was they seemed quite preoccupied with this docudrama they were working on, so I had to bide my time to scream sense at them between takes. Well, we all bonded and Dave was particularly interested in talking to me about a documentary. *This is great!* We had lunch. We had lunch again. Of course, the more Dave talked, the more I realised that maybe this documentary isn't going to get made after all. The main reason was money. Apparently, you need money to do these kinds of things. Sure, there was funding, but it didn't seem very clear that there would be funding available for a Cromwell in Ireland documentary – particularly since they had already done one in recent years. FFS.

I was totally convinced that I needed to get to a wider audience in order for Cromwell's exoneration to have any chance of making it in the wider world. I was also convinced that others would come after me and pick up where I left off, but bollocks to that. I want to make as much of an impression as I can myself – while I'm still here! Still alive.

A novel you say, eh? But isn't that, like, fiction?

Another new idea. So, I was just after finishing a Parkrun one Saturday morning. Did I mention that I'm an obsessive runner yet? No? Aw, there's another book in that! And after some of my reasonably entertaining race reports had appeared on a certain Facebook page, one of the runners (Damon O'Shea for the record) said to me that I should write a novel. Now, I didn't even read fiction, so how could I even begin to write a novel? But I strangely found myself in true Homer Simpson style saying, 'I'll do it!'

Crazy, maybe. But the idea began to gnaw away at me. A novel, eh? But what would I write about? Then it hit me. You should always write about what you know. Because that's what they say you should always do when you're going to write a novel. Yes! You got it in one. Running! I would write about running! Naw, it had to be Cromwell. But what form should the novel take? How do I even...what? I had nothing. So, after Googling a bit I hared down to Waterstones in Drogheda and bought a few Hilary Mantel novels and one or two more historical fiction books by people who seemed to know what they were doing. Ominously it looked like you had to be a good researcher. Being really good at writing seemed to be another major factor. I was neither and I knew it. But I wasn't going to let complete incompetence stop me. Well, it never stopped me before. My imagination ran wild. Up to now I had been writing academic books – that are not in the least bit academic. But they definitely fit into the non-fiction category. Fiction, you say? Why, that would mean a totally different audience. Hmm, I might just throw a bit of sex in there. Seemed to me that all good novels need to have a bit of durt, so mine was not going to be an exception. Here was a way I could get to the masses. God, I'm such a naive bastard. There's a lot of fricken masses out there.

The Protector is born

A year later and *The Protector: The Fall and Rise of Oliver Cromwell* was born. It was a lockdown book. I started it on 1 January 2021, and I finished it in May. I sent the manuscript off to my old pals John Hunt Publishing and they responded with a contract. Sure, I make it sound easy. But it isn't at all easy. Because of the modest but adequate sales from *Cromwell Was Framed*, I had managed to convince the lovely people at JHP that I was worth taking a punt on, and that's really all it amounts to.

The book was a fictional biography. I called it 'faction'. The story practically told itself. He was born. He did some shit. He died. At the time of writing it's probably too early to say that it's an abject failure as a novel, but it did get to the Number 1 spot on Amazon in its category just immediately after its release in June 2022. So, for now the jury's out on that one.

Dan! Dan! Dan! Dan! Dan! Dan! Dan! Dan! Dan! Dan! Dan! Dan! Dan! Dan!

During the publication process I was having a conversation with a friend of mine, who is a history teacher and who said he would prefer not to be named, Ryan McMahon from Castleblayney in Monaghan. I don't get to discuss Cromwell with history teachers often, so I asked Ryan what the schoolbooks were saying about Cromwell these days. After all my hard work, and the work of more discerning historians, I was pretty sure that he would tell me that the education system had gotten with the times and here now, in 2022, they were a lot more circumspect in what they were teaching children. What Ryan had to say totally blew my mind. 'Well,' he said, 'there's this book that was published in 2018 by CJ Fallon called *History in Focus*, written by Dan Sheedy, and you're not gonna like it.' Or words to that effect. Clearly, I'm paraphrasing now because I can't remember the *exact* conversation. Ryan scanned the offending page of the book – which is directed at 12- to 15-year-olds – and when I saw it I nearly fell off the high moral ground that I had bought and paid for years ago. Okay – here it comes – after 25 years of trying to change the country's perception of Ollie's deeds, somewhere down the country one Dan Sheedy sat down in the last few years to write the following words:

After he landed in Dublin, Cromwell carried out some of the most brutal military operations in the history of Ireland. [So far, so good. That's actually not bad at all. I would even change 'some of the most' to '*the* most brutal' military operations in the history of Ireland.]

But Dan didn't stop there. Here comes the kicker:

His New Model Army laid siege to Drogheda in September 1649. Following victory in the siege, his forces entered the town and proceeded to massacre 3,500 of its inhabitants. Cromwell repeated the act during and after the Siege of Wexford in October that same year, when a further 4,000 people were killed.

Good man, Dan. Three and a half thousand of Drogheda's inhabitants. No soldiers at all now. It's actually backwards we're going. While the figure of dead soldiers at Wexford is traditionally seen as 1,500, Dan threw in a wide net of 'during and after the siege', concocting a new figure of 4,000. But even worse than that – now they were people. Of course. Soldiers are people. Well, apart from some of the characters in *The Lord of the Rings* who were more akin to leprechauns. But the word 'people' conjures up images of civilian atrocities, does it not? Or am I overthinking this again? My bollix, I'm overthinking it.

I was incensed, outsensed, upsensed, downsensed to the point where I could no longer see any sense. Good holy mother of divine shite. Yes, people, there is a new evil abroad. A hideous menace that threatens world peace. A sinister power that will wreak havoc unless these words are cast deep into the fires of Mount Doom. But who now can save the world from this awful peril? I needed to get my flying underpants and superhero tights out of the drawer and swing into action!

The publisher responds

I e-mailed the publisher, CJ Fallon, and I told him how wide of the mark Sheedy's words were. I even quoted the Yeats thing about the 'fanatic hearts'. And I explained how little hearts all over the country would now be infused with anti-English hatred. I wondered if he really wanted that sort of blood on his hands, in so many words.

I got a reply from a Fintan Lane, who was extremely courteous. Here are his words verbatim:

Dear Tom,

Apropos the Cromwellian period, we prefer to lean on the research of historians such as Micheál Ó Siochrú, Pádraig Lenihan, and others, but thank you for the interesting correspondence and I wish you the very best of luck with your forthcoming publication.

I suppose I could have left it there, but the fact that he had said that they 'leaned on' the research of my two old adversaries fascinated me. Wow. Because we've already seen that neither of these historians had ever said such a thing – that Sheedy was espousing. I've quoted their research conclusions here already. Three and a half thousand dead civilians at Drogheda. Four thousand dead 'people' at Wexford! I'm actually running out of words now. I really tried not to be patronised by the publisher's response but I didn't make a good job of that.

Anyhoo, this gets more interesting. I decided to reply to Fintan and because I love to stir the shit, I actually copied Pádraig Lenihan and Micheál Ó Siochrú on my reply, so they would get to see this gross misinterpretation of their research at first hand too. In my pragmatic world where common sense should really prevail (but rarely does) I fully expected them to chip in to the debate and alert Fintan to the error the publishers and the writer had clearly made. And we'd all live happily ever after.

Lies, lies and damned lies

Yep, you've guessed it – nothing. They said nothing – as far as I know anyway. Independently, I e-mailed my good friend Professor Lenihan to ask him what I was missing here and how could he casually allow this to happen. Fair play to him, he replied to me, but his response was extremely disappointing, and we agreed to differ. This whole episode badly shook my faith in human nature. There's just no way that the work of these two guys could be interpreted the way Sheedy interpreted it. It got me wondering what world these people lived in at all. Surely the integrity of historical interpretation is what's paramount here. How could they all be so casual when they know deep inside children are still being taught lies? Lies that create 'fanatic hearts' as W.B. Yeats told us clearly enough. Here in 2023?!

I couldn't let it go. I let some time pass and I e-mailed Fintan Lane again. By now he was ignoring me. I e-mailed him again. Nothing. Then I decided to check out what the protocols were regarding the publishing of history books for schools. I soon discovered a booklet available to publishers and writers of these books, *Guidelines for Teachers* (History, Leaving Certificate), from the Department of Education and the National Council for Curriculum and Assessment.

The guidelines read:

The emphasis on available evidence is also of key importance. Evidence is the grist to the historian's mill; without evidence there is no basis to historical judgements and the historian's questions must hang in the air until sources of evidence are unearthed.

Okay, guys. This is so wrong it beggars belief. I really couldn't stand idly by and let this continue. I e-mailed Fintan Lane again and I asked him to meet with me. No response. I discovered who the Managing Director of CJ Fallon was – a John Gilsenan – and I e-mailed him too to see if that would make any difference. It didn't. I was a pariah. An amateur who hadn't a clue and who deserved none of their time. Now, I suppose it's possible that none of these e-mails got through to these people and if that's the case then I apologise for misinterpreting their intentions, which may well have been honourable. But on the face of it, this looked for all the world like they were ignoring me.

I then pored over an e-mail to the National Council for Curriculum and Assessment for hours and sent it to them through their website. No reply.

Frustrated, I decided to contact the Minister for Education, Norma Foley. Surely somebody somewhere would be able to help with this! Well, I got a reply from Derek Newcombe, the minister's Private Secretary, which was nice of Derek, but no good to me really. I suppose I just contacted the minister to say that I had contacted the minister. The way things were looking, I didn't expect instant retribution. Derek outlined that the 'current policy within the Department of Education is not to endorse any particular product or publication, including textbooks. In terms of the content, the Department of Education does not have a role in endorsing any content in any educational textbook.' Yada. Yada. Yada.

Feck *The Protector* – here comes *The Guardian*

But then in August 2022 came a little chink of light. Due to an upcoming book that was to be published in September of the entire writings and speeches of Oliver Cromwell up to date, *The Observer* and *The Guardian* ran a piece on Cromwell. The headline read, 'Has history got it all wrong on Cromwell's hostility to Catholics?' The journalist, Donna Ferguson, had interviewed historian John Morrill for the article. If you remember, John was a little all over the place when it came to me. On one hand he had initially e-mailed me to say he agreed with me that there were no civilians killed in cold blood, then some years later he completely castigated my work when he supported Jason McElligott in an article he wrote when he said, and I repeat:

Jason McElligott has given us an outstanding summary of the nationalist and revisionist cases and a totally convincing and necessary explanation of why Tom Reilly's claim that there was no civilian massacre at Drogheda is not to be trusted. In essence Reilly fails the test of source criticism at almost every turn. Despite Tom Reilly's attempt to minimise the number of civilian deaths, there can be no doubt that they took place.

Thanks, John. Way to ruin my hopes and dreams. It makes me wonder now how you can justify this next quote, but then again I'm just an amateur, sure what would I know?

Anyway, John is now quoted as saying in *The Guardian* that in Ireland:

Cromwell thinks that persecution is always counterproductive because when you target militants you finish by radicalizing moderates. He also believes that the way to convert people is not by persecution but by kindness.

As for the long declaration that Cromwell wrote in Youghal when he was really pissed off, which I've alluded to already, Morrill and his co-authors had discovered earlier versions of it. Morrill says:

The new versions we found make it clear that while Cromwell is severely critical of the Irish clergy for stimulating rebellion and supporting the massacre of protestants, he is trying to demonstrate to the ordinary people of Ireland that they have nothing to fear from him.

Ironic, eh? What can I tell ya.

What was that? *The Guardian*? Again?

In September 2022, while I was idly picking my feet in some local restaurant or other, I came across an article from *The Guardian* that was entitled 'Killing Leprechauns: Irish satirist mines British ignorance in comedy podcast'. The reporter was one Rory Carroll, and the piece was about comedian/impressionist Oliver Callan. None of these things are relevant really, except to say that Rory went a bit mad with his introduction.

'When Oliver Cromwell's forces sacked the Irish town of Drogheda in 1649 and massacred its inhabitants, the comedy potential seemed limited,' he began. 'Thousands perished and that was just the start of a military campaign that wiped out much of Ireland's population before Cromwell returned to England.'

I didn't really care what the rest of the article had to say and as you might imagine I shot off a terse yet hilarious e-mail to Rory telling him that he was wrong. I do that a lot, as you'll have noticed.

Well, I had clearly piqued Rory's interest and eventually he agreed that this might be worth a story. On 26 November *The Observer* and *The Guardian* published a piece that the sub-editor beautifully called, 'Irish amateur historian on lonely mission to save bogeyman Cromwell from genocide charges'. After 25 years I was still on a lonely mission, and I had clearly made no impression at all on Rory. Well, fair dinkum. The uphill battle continues. Mind you, after that headline, I felt like I was back at the very start of all this. What the hell does that say about my country? Are we really that bigoted? Obviously, the answer is yes. We really are. Historians of Ireland, hang your heads in abject shame.

The hook for Rory was the fact that elsewhere in Ireland at that very time, John Morrill, Micheál Ó Siochrú and other notable early modern luminaries were launching the entire collection of Cromwell's letters and speeches in the third iteration of such a work, the previous being by Thomas Carlyle and Wilbur Cortez Abbott. I didn't hold out any real hope that the boys would suddenly come to their senses and suddenly agree with me. And I was completely right. In *God's Executioner*, and elsewhere, Ó Siochrú makes the claim that it was impossible for the attacking New Model Army at Drogheda to differentiate between combatants and non-combatants.

So let's talk about Drogheda in 1649 for a second. I have read and re-read the Drogheda Corporation records over many years. There are centuries of records. I have written about them. I still research and read them for local studies. I understand that the town's inhabitants were tenaciously Protestant and fiercely adherent to London, whoever was in power at this particular period in history and right up to the late nineteenth century.

During the mid-seventeenth century, like all urban centres on these islands, no doubt loyalties in Drogheda were divided. We have evidence of this. We know about the Lady Wilmot plot, for instance, to allow Cromwell access to the town. Conversely, we also know that some Catholics turfed some Protestants out of St Peter's and had mass said there. I would contend that there were a lot more Catholics in the town during the siege than normally as the defenders were made up of Catholic and Protestant royalists.

Drogheda was within the Pale. Parliaments were held there. The town had resisted the Catholic Irish Rebellion forces of Phelim O'Neill for five months just eight short years earlier. Essentially, what I'm trying to say is that the citizens of the town did not represent the enemy within for the New Model in that it was not a typically Irish Catholic town. Demographically, Drogheda was far more akin to Dublin – also in the Pale – in its make-up, both in religious and political allegiances and also culturally. The inhabitants of the latter had nothing to fear from Cromwell's army, so the same could easily be said about Drogheda. On the face of it, then, the children of Drogheda who, as Wood claims, were allegedly held up as shields did not represent enemy (Catholic) children. In the same way, women dressed up to the nines who were allegedly murdered were not automatically enemy (Catholic) women.

I would not make the same point about Wexford, a resolutely Catholic/royalist enclave which declared for the Confederacy very early on in the wars, nailing its colours firmly to the Ormond/king's mast. In fact, had the Wood tract been recounting these events about Wexford, it would be much more difficult to dismiss. A New Model on the rampage in Wexford might well have had the capacity to do what Wood alleges. But Drogheda was *very* different. The most professional army of its time, the New Model had no motivation to kill the unarmed innocents of Drogheda. The fact that their explicit orders from Cromwell were also to the contrary, to me, is simply academic.

To suggest that the soldiers just ran amok is simply a ridiculous assertion. Moreover, to suggest that it was difficult to tell the difference between civilians and soldiers is fairly mad. Bandoliers, swords, pikes, muskets and whatever other weapons the defenders had in their hands clearly meant they would have been 'in arms' and therefore on the death list. If, as Ó Siochrú claims, the attackers just randomly killed anything that moved in Drogheda, friend or foe – then why did they not just randomly kill the inhabitants of Dublin? Facetious, I know, they didn't attack Dublin; but you get my point. Drogheda was a mirror of Dublin at that time.

Telly again. I'm high-flyin' now

Now, elsewhere in my life I'm a big fan of Michael Portillo. Not the politician aspect of his life, because I haven't got a clue about that – I just love the vibe that comes off the telly when I watch his railway journeys. I think he's a wonderful presenter. Anyway, it transpired that Michael, or one of his minions, had seen the piece in *The Observer*. I got an e-mail from GBN News. I had never even heard of the actual channel, but that's completely academic. Turns out Michael does a Sunday morning show that features politics, current affairs, culture and art. I wasn't sure exactly what category I was to appear in, but I really didn't care. I was going to be that gobshite who was on the telly again. I was asked to travel to the London studios, and I was perfectly willing to go. The bright lights of the studio beckoned. However, in the days before the show the weather gods played havoc with flying conditions and instead we agreed that we would do a Zoom thing.

I was really looking forward to being interviewed by Michael as I knew he loved history. We were bound to have the craic. They asked me to send some images of my book covers as well, and there was no reason for me not to, so I did. On the Saturday before the show, I decided to contact a few historians who I actually have relationships with to let them know that I was going to be on. Well, I figured, how often is there a Cromwell conversation on national TV? I was pretty sure they'd like to know. I certainly would have, if the shoe was on the other hand.

TV producers playing tricks

One of the historians I e-mailed was Prof. Ronald Hutton. Straight away he came back and revealed that he, too, was to appear on the very same show. Well, that's a turn-up for the books, I thought to myself. The producers never mentioned that there were going to be two of us. I figured out that they wanted to try to blindside me. Clearly a media trick to catch the likes of me off guard. When we went 'live' the next day, they did it beautifully. I was introduced by Michael and immediately his tone inferred that I was to be stunned by the appearance of a real historian, Prof. Ronald Hutton, who appeared on the screen next to me. Hilarious. These are the kinds of things TV people do. I had already forgiven Michael and his crew the previous day. In fact during the debate I set Michael up brilliantly – if I do say so myself – when I went on and on and then said that I would challenge any historian anywhere to try to break down my arguments in Cromwell's favour, whereupon he brought in the good professor...

Of course, Ronald Hutton was a poor adversary. We made for bad sparring partners, mainly due to the fact that he fundamentally agreed with my research – with the exception of one significant piece of evidence: THOMAS à WOOD!

Oh! My! God!

And now, ladies and gentlemen, I come to the biggest drumroll moment of this book to date. This is simply fannytastic. And what's more, I'm telling you this exactly as it happened in chronological order.

One of the other history experts I contacted that Saturday to let him know about the *Michael Portillo Show* was one military historian by the name of James Scott Wheeler. Now, Scott and I have been irregular communicants over the years as he wrote the definitive book on Cromwell in Ireland called *Cromwell in Ireland*. See what I did there? Like *Honourable Enemy*, it also came out in 1999. At the time, neither of us knew that we were each writing about the exact same topic, albeit mine being super-controversial and a bit all over the shop, and his being an actual real, insightful academic narrative. Scott also kindly agreed to write an essay for *Cromwell and Ireland: New Perspectives*. So we have what constitutes an excellent working relationship.

Anyway, Scott came back to me that day and told me that he was currently in the process of researching more about Drogheda. He was doing a piece for an upcoming publication that was drilling into the detail about just exactly who was killed at Drogheda. In other words, he was dealing head-on with the civilian massacre stories. This was great! I knew that Scott, as an American, had no axe to grind and would be looking at this whole thing quite dispassionately. But even better was to come.

'This Wood evidence,' said Scott. 'I've just discovered that Wood might not have been in Drogheda at all during the 1649 siege.'

Well, shiver me timbers, slap me silly and call me an unkey's muncle. My gob was completely smacked. What did you just say, Scott? Wood mightn't even have been at Drogheda?! Holy lantern Jaysus!

Okay, here we go. Here are the very words of one James Scott Wheeler, a real historian.

Referring to our old friend Father Murphy, Scott states:

Murphy used the account (Wood) which claimed that Wood was a soldier in Colonel Ingoldsby's regiment at Drogheda. However, Ingoldsby's regiment was not in Ireland on 11 September 1649 but instead was stationed at garrisons in Oxford and Bristol, England. It was also not one of the formations selected for service in Ireland with Cromwell in the spring and summer of 1649.

Charles Firth's *Regimental History of Cromwell's Army* notes that Henry Ingoldsby volunteered for duty in Ireland 'and tried in vain to persuade his regiment to follow his example'. He (Ingoldsby) did serve under Cromwell at the siege of Ross in October 1649 and he may have been at Drogheda. He received a command of a regiment of dragoons in June 1650. One of his officers was Thomas Wood, who served as a troop commander under him.

Well, God bless us and save us, said old Missus Davis, I never knew herrings was fish! This is incredible stuff. How come nobody ever found this out before? So, Ingoldsby's regiment wasn't even in Drogheda when Cromwell attacked it! So it's most likely that Wood wasn't there either! I don't know what to say. I have no words. Naturally, I couldn't help myself and I revealed to Ronald that Wood might not have even been in Drogheda on the *Michael Portillo Show*. Just for the drama! Y'know yourself.

And before we finish on Scott. Modesty prevents me from taking the full credit for coining Toby Barnard's phrase 'an honourable enemy', which is completely his; but I will anyway: in the 'conclusions' of his essay, Scott Wheeler says the following about Drogheda:

> Cromwell did not order a massacre of unarmed townspeople. Claims that there was a widespread killing of innocent civilians is not supported by the contemporary accounts. Furthermore, compared to most of the military commanders who led forces in Ireland from 1641 to 1653, Cromwell was 'an honourable enemy'.

Ah, now here. So, if anyone's ever looking for me, I'll be beyant in Americae living out the rest of my days with my new bestest friend in the whole wide world, James Scott Wheeler. Now was that so hard, young Ó Siochrú? You getting this, McElligott? How about you, Morrill? Lenihan? Anything to say? Yep. It just gets worser and worser for you guys. It's just such a bitch that nobody will ever read this book. Least of all, you four. But if this book ever reaches posterity, whatever the hell that is, and somebody simply happens upon it, well, you guys in the future will know now that this massacre was made up! Hey – you bastards in posterity! Amn't I brilliant?!

So, what's the real story behind Wood then?

We may never really know what the Wood tract is all about. But I do know that it's quite a stretch to call the words of Thomas's brother Anthony, written quite a number of years later, an eyewitness account. Considering the way Wood's life was cobbled together as a book, my suggestion that it could have been altered by other hands is clearly conceivable. Until somebody points out significant flaws in my methodology, I will continue to dismiss Wood. But if reasonable arguments were proffered to justify my dismissal of all the other writers and participants that say nothing of civilian deaths, then I would dismiss them all and accept Wood. Essentially for me – it's Wood versus the others. Turns out he probably wasn't even in Drogheda at the time!

My best guess is that as a royalist, Anthony Wood simply adhered to the Restoration norms, which was to obliterate the republic in all its forms and to castigate Cromwell at every turn. He had a brother who fought under Cromwell at some stage. Such kudos. The stories he could tell. This was a time when the horrendous massacre of the soldiery at Drogheda was beginning to morph into the massacre of civilians by that usurper Cromwell. Imagine the attention Wood might get for regaling audiences with sensationalised gory detail – either Thomas or Anthony. Take your pick. It may well have been one of hundreds of stories about Drogheda that did the rounds in Restoration England, and he decided to include it in his memoirs for conspiratorial reasons. Many other stories of a similar nature probably never made it into print, but I can imagine the fireside stories about Drogheda growing with hyperbole and embellishment as the years passed and it was an acceptable pastime to condemn Cromwell. Sure, everybody was doing it.

In short – for me, Wood's melodramatic story seems carefully crafted to shock and it certainly does that. Had it been much less salacious and slightly more plausible I might view it differently.

On the other side is the deafening silence of the hundreds of others who witnessed the events (escapees) and the hundreds of others who spoke to them.

But fair play to Scott Wheeler. What an incredible revelation!

Hutton completely humbles me

Fresh from his appearance on TV with me, Prof. Ronald Hutton surfaced again soon afterwards. To all intensive purposes (shuddup, I know!) I'm a fan of his and he's *somewhat* of a fan of mine. Unlike many others, he acknowledges the work I've done on Cromwell, and from an academic of such gargantuan proportions, this to me is massive. The first volume of his magnum opus, *The Making of Oliver Cromwell*, was published in 2022 to wide acclaim.

So you can imagine my surprise when one day, as I was idly picking my feet at my laptop, I received an e-mail from him telling me that he would be happy to have me critique his chapter on Ireland before it was published in volume 2. So, what's happening now exactly? Somebody who actually respects my work? Wants me to check his academic narrative?! To be fair I had literally bombarded him with my opinions on the events at Drogheda when I heard that he was writing about it, and he always graciously accepted my completely unsolicited overtures.

But when I got this particular e-mail! Well, I don't mind saying I was completely blown away by this and I had a total 'pinch myself' moment. What an incredible breath of fresh air! I tried to remain cool and calm, and wanted to say, 'Sure, Ron, just bang it over to me and I'll get to it when I have time.' I didn't. No point in pissing off another academic with vernacular like that. Besides, the utter eloquence of the man demanded a certain reciprocal articulacy.

The chapter arrived. It was beautiful. Mesmerising. I loved it. I wanted to wine and dine it. I wanted to whisper sweet nothings in its ear. I wanted to go to bed with it and do unspeakable things to it. While I was intimately acquainted with the details of the subject matter, it was like I was reading about Cromwell in Ireland for the very first time. I was even mentioned in the text! We exchanged views and went off on our separate merry ways. I couldn't convince him about Wood and that was disappointing. But hey, it's all a question of interpretation. I think that what we're essentially saying now is that the evidence for *any number* of civilian deaths has no solid evidential basis and instead we must rely on interpretations, or as I like to call it – speculation. This is quite a distance from the stuff children are *still* being taught in Ireland today. I was certainly the better for the exchange. I can't speak for Prof. Hutton, but he was now my new hero. Could we really be slowly getting there?

I have a dream

There may be many twists and turns along the way on this journey in whatever time I have left in me auld mortal coil and I'm looking forward to them all. Clearly I have only highlighted my experiences to date. No doubt during the year-long publication process for this book other shit will have gone down and I will have both received and delivered many a blow. But that's all gonna be in my next volume which I will probably call *Saint Oliver Cromwell*.

I fully expect to be awarded an OBE or an MBE, or even a bumblebee would do, for my services to Anglo-Irish relations. Suffice to say it's been a pretty lonely journey. I've taken a lot of flak, and by jingo I expect to be taking a lot more before I clop my pogs.

But seriously, folks, I'm not actually on drugs. I've come close, but I have not yet crossed the Rubicon of hopelessness. Can we please stop teaching seventeenth-century propaganda to kids, students of all ages, adults, pensioners – *everybody*! Right now I dream of a day when we embrace the facts. I dream of a time when Cromwell is seen in an accurate historical context when it comes to Ireland. I dream of a day when we stop judging the past with our twenty-first-century eyes. I dream of a wrinkle cream that actually works on todgers. People, I have spread my dreams under your feet. Tread softly, because you tread on my dreams.

Chapter 8

2023

So, seriously, like, where did the massacre myth originally come from?

If the Oliver Cromwell civilian massacre myth that has infected Anglo-Irish relations for the last four odd centuries was a noise that could be measured in decibels it would be like standing beside a speaker at an ACDC concert. Or camping in a volcano as it exploded its fiery intestines on the world below. Or listening to the missus singing in the shower. Horrendously deafening is the only way to properly explain it. If you're Irish, this noise comes from all directions: the womb, the cradle, school, home, work, church, pub, college, the streets, the roads, the boreens and even the whispering grass throughout the four green fields of Ireland. It's a freight train of commotion, a juggernaut of sound that has travelled across the centuries with its horn perpetually blaring.

Bastard Brits. Practically anybody who is Irish will swear on their mother's grave that Cromwell massacred the ordinary unarmed people of Ireland. *Ochón agus ochón.* Sure, it was probably screaming at me in every chapter of Peig Sayers that I never read at school. And didn't Oliver Cromwell even bate the shite out of our hero Fionn McCool and all of na Fianna with a blackthorn shillelagh he stole from Kate Kearney's Cottage below in Killarney? And then sure didn't he batter Diarmuid *agus* Gráinne to death with their own hurleys? Yes indeed. He's blamed for everything. He also hung, drew and quartered Saint Oliver Plunkett with an elastic he got in a lucky bag.

The civilian massacre tradition is cemented into Irish history in the same way as the old tale of the Children of Lír shoving wads of shamrock up the brown bull of Cooley's arse on Michael

Collins' farm below in Cork on a soft day, thang God, top of the mornin' t'ya. The Oliver Cromwell civilian massacre story is more Irish than the Irish themselves. How could it not be true? Story over. Case closed.

But it happens *not* to be true. Based on the actual available evidence, that is. But in order to dismantle it, we need to go back and understand where it all came from. And how did these stories gain such incredible traction?

Okay – let's have a total recall

Just for pig, imagine if you can the following scenario, however unlikely it might seem.

Time check: July 1649. Place check: Drogheda, Ireland. The long, hot summer is in full swing. The old medieval town on the banks of the Boyne is a little past its prime. Mind you, the ancient high defensive walls that had been built in 1234 kept the Irish bastards out back in 1641 when they surrounded the town for five months, throwing all sorts of shapes. Feckin' Irish gits. This is an English town. Don't people realise that?

The locals didn't want to hand the place over to the Irish. It was a long time since the Anglo-Normans colonised the Boyneside site and built the town on it, and they had lived there happily ever after since. No Irish rabble on a doomed rebellion crusade were going to take this place away from them! The king beyant in London was their master then and always.

Well, okay, parliament had just chopped the head off the king, so the situation wasn't exactly ideal. That's true. Now, as we cut into history at this precise moment, as a result of the headless king we had two opposing sides on these islands. Those who supported parliament. And those who supported the deceased king's son – also called Charles – who was 19 years old at this time. His balls had well dropped, and he was well capable of becoming a teenage king. But at this particular moment he was in exile. Or as the roundheads used to say about him, it could be worse, he could be reigning.

The real peeps of Drawda

Within the walls of the town of Drogheda on 10 July 1649, all of the seventeenth-century trades were represented: the vomit collectors, the rat catchers, the shit shovelers, the monkey spankers, the sheep shaggers etc. By this time I think they no longer shat out their bedroom windows onto the streets below, but otherwise life in the town was quite rudimentary and bordering on the very stinky. (If you think you're having it tough with the energy crisis, read a history book!) Politically, economically and culturally, Drogheda was a quintessential seventeenth-century town.

There's somebody at the door!

So now you just have to imagine that the inhabitants were all going about their daily business that lovely July day. Imagine the scene. Imagine what the population were getting up to. The flies were around shite, the town drunks were pissing in your door, you might have been a leper whose knob had just fallen off during an over-enthusiastic wank, and if you were in the lower echelons of society you probably had to wipe your own arse with your *own* bare hand. Assuming that hadn't fallen off as well. Urban seventeenth-century bliss. Drawda. At the cutting edge of modernity. All was right with the world.

Suddenly, outside the walls an attacking army arrived at the gates of the town and there was quite the hullabaloo. The initial stages were tense. Shots were fired. Shit went down. Many of the protagonists' parentage was called into serious question. War brought out the worst in people. These were strange times indeed. But again? Seriously? Did we not just do this in 1641? Were the Irish out there again? With delusions of victory? Nah, the townsfolk realised pretty quickly that whoever it was at the gates it definitely wasn't the Irish. There was a different foe trying to get in now.

In Ireland the row between the roundheads and the cavaliers had superseded anything the Irish had to offer by this time. The inhabitants were obviously happy that the town was well defended by its defenders. The military regiments above on the battlements had been there for two long years. So they knew the town well by this time. They had bought milk in the local shops for their tea. No doubt, they had drunk ale in the local taverns and shagged many of the local wenches, and maybe even the local non-binary boutique owners. Some of them may have even joined the local knitting fraternity. Who knows what levels of involvement the military defenders had gotten up to with the local yokels. But whatever it was, they were stout defenders of the cause and consequently stout defenders of the walls of Drogheda at this time. Thank feck for that. No attacking army was gonna breach these walls any time soon!

But hark! What's this? The two opposing generals were in discussions at the walls. Maybe there won't be another siege. Relations seemed to be extremely cordial. No point in spoiling a lovely summer's day with a bit of an auld bloodbath, now is there? The sky was blue, temperatures were high, and that sun wasn't gonna soak itself up. Surely they could make time for an afternoon on the beach. But in reality the discussions were tense. The testosterone levels were through the roof. The two sides were quite far apart when it came to their ideals. There was a lot of eff you-ing and 'are you startin'?'

Was all hell about to break loose? Or was common sense about to prevail?

Okay, calm the feck down, this is not what you think it is

If you're still with me, I need to make a confession at this point in the narrative. See, I'm just setting the scene here to completely lull you into a false sense of lunacy. If you're an idiot, which you clearly are, you'll have fallen completely into my trap. This was *not* Cromwell arriving at Drogheda. At this very moment in history (10 July 1649) Oliver Cromwell was still beyant in London packing his socks and jocks and a few cheeky strawberry-flavoured condoms in preparation for his Ireland odyssey with the boys. True story.

Read this and weep

And the kicker in this? The defenders of Drogheda that very day – and for the two previous years – were *parliamentarian* soldiers. Roundheads. Anti-royalists. King haters. Cromwell's own men! You getting this? If he had had the benefit of a Ryanair flight from Stansted and if he had arrived on that exact day (10th July), he could have strolled through the gates of the town without a bye or a leave because effectively, having accepted the role as leader of the parliamentarian army in Ireland a few weeks earlier (Lord Lieutenant of Ireland), the town of Drogheda was completely under his control on that day!

Now, I'd love to repeat that last paragraph so it sinks in, but some bastard up ahead in the book production process will probably edit it out. They don't like repetition. They don't like repetition. So I won't. Instead, I'd respectfully suggest that you read it again. Take your time. And just so I can finish off my seismic point on this issue, you might wanna read this next bit again too.

The confrontation at the walls of Drogheda on 10 July 1649 was between Oliver Cromwell's parliamentarian defenders of the town and the royalist attackers. Discussions were indeed held between both sides, and the town was captured by the royalists as a result. Indeed, many of the parliamentarian defenders changed to the royalist side that day. Who knows why. Pay and conditions? Benefits? Double time on a Sunday and bank holidays? Bonuses? A pension? A working-from-home programme? Equal pay?

Whatever the reason, we also know that many of the parliamentarian soldiers who had been in the town went back to Dublin (the regiment of Colonel Michael Jones) that day, and then when Cromwell arrived in August, these same men were subsumed by the army he had brought with him. That same army, with those same men who had been in Drogheda for months, if not years, very soon found themselves outside the walls of Drogheda with Cromwell, trying to get back in. And just in case you're missing this – if these guys had spent time in Drogheda fraternising with the local population, drinking their milk and riding their women, how effen likely is it that they would now massacre them all in cold blood. Eh? Eh? Do me one.

So just to cap that off: the next day, on 11 July 1649, Oliver Cromwell departed London en route to Bristol with a milk-white standard raised above his entourage. Everyone wanted peace, and by Jaysus they were going to fight a god-awful and bloody war to get it.

So why was he even here in the first place?

Following his most unlikely, yet spectacular, string of victories in the first and second civil wars in England, Oliver Cromwell arrived in Ireland on 15 August 1649 at the head of a flotilla of 35 ships carrying a level of ordnance never before seen in Ireland. His reputation had arrived well before him. He entered a chaotic, multifarious landscape that was already war-torn and desolate. Earlier in the decade, as we've seen, the Irish rebellion had broken out.

Soon afterwards, parliament had fallen out with their king, Charles I. The English then became embroiled in a bitter war among themselves. After parliament executed Charles I, Cromwell's imperatives in Ireland were to quash the potential of an Irish/Catholic army joining forces with the young sex-mad Prince Charles. Cromwell was also to ensure that the investments of those English adventurers, who had pledged money to the army for the subjugation of Ireland in return for land, would mature. He would ultimately be successful on both counts. Cromwell's enemies in Ireland were anyone who was pro-king and anti-parliament. These were unprecedented times. Parliament had no lawful basis on which to rule, but due to their military conquests they were clearly in control. The staunch Protestant, the Earl of Ormond, effectively led whatever resistance Cromwell would encounter on Irish soil.

And now that the royalists were in control of Drogheda, he needed to take it back. It was the gateway to the North and – according to all the history books I've read – militarily it was located in a very strategic position.

Context. Y'can't bate a bit of context

So now just a little bit of context about the main man himself. The Catholic hater. The destroyer of Drogheda and Wexford. Among the many and various accusations that have been levelled against the former Cambridgeshire farmer is the allegation that he hated Catholicism, or *potpourri* as it was often called at that time for some odd reason. While this is a multilayered issue, such a glib contention does not represent Cromwell's views accurately, as the evidence patently shows. Indeed, some would argue that he held a moralistic position that would be difficult to argue with today.

Popes throughout the ages ordered their flocks to indiscriminately massacre ordinary people all over the world, if they did not conform to the Christian faith: the crusades, the persecution of the Cathars in France, Jews and Muslims virtually throughout history, the inquisitions etc., etc. Despite extolling virtue and kindness in its teaching, church leadership has spearheaded a long history of outright murderous depravity. To some degree this was more like Satanism. Then again Satanism is purely a kind of disease of Christianity. You've really got to be a Christian to believe in Satan. I'm not a big fan of Satan or the idea of being in hell forever. Eternity's a terrible thought – I mean where is it all going to end?

These lunatic popes! I mean it is virtually impossible not to feel sympathy for the Cathars in southern France who were wiped out (slaughtered in cold blood, men, women and children) during the Albigensian Crusade on the orders of Pope Innocent III simply because they did not conform to the Roman Church. Indulgences didn't help the Church's case. Many bishops saw them as an easy way to get rich as they extorted money from people in exchange for the promise of eternal life or the release of loved ones from Purgatory. The legacy of the inquisitions, where you either converted or were executed, is another horror invented and ruthlessly implemented by the Catholic Church. It is difficult also to imagine that Oliver Cromwell was unaware of the exploits of Johann Tserclaes, the Catholic Count of Tilly fighting for the Holy Roman Empire, who was responsible for the deaths of 25,000 Protestant civilians at Magdeburg on 20 May 1631, during the Tutty Years' War.

Cromwell was also of the opinion that it was the Catholic clergy – and no other entity – who had stirred the impressionable native Irish into the rebellion of 1641, and it was they who were directly responsible for the 'horrid massacres' (his words) of innocent Protestants that ensued. These were the same Irish who appeared before the walls of Drogheda in 1641. So you can imagine how the town's inhabitants would have shat themselves.

These are the things with which Oliver Cromwell's school lessons bristled in the town of his birth, Huntingdon, Cambridgeshire, in the early 1600s. The gunpowder plot in 1605, when he was just 6 years old, was organised by Catholics, another reason why they would be seen in a negative light throughout England. Yet, as Lord Protector, Cromwell fostered a policy of religious toleration and professed often that he would not 'meddle with any man's conscience', Catholics included. For my part? If God wanted us to believe in him, he'd effen exist!

So, anyway, where was I?

Okay, so back to the story. Remember? It's August 1649. Here he was in Dublin. Apart from taking a well-earned dump on *terra firma*, what's the first thing that he did after he got off the boat? Anybody? He issued that decree that unarmed civilians were not to be harmed by any of the officers and soldiers under his command – on pain of death. Again, I feel like repeating that, but y'know what these editors are like. Y'know what these editors are like.

The weather during the week preceding the siege was shite. The New Model Army began to set up camp on the south side of the town, overlooking the Dale and beyant to St Mary's Church of Ireland. Some skirmishes took place in the first few days in the Platin Road, Clinton's Lane, Coolagh Street area of the town, which was then open ground. That's just really information for locals. Like he was to do later at Wexford, Ormond gave orders to have 'all superfluous people' evacuated from the town.

Pause here to take that in. Got it?
Cool, now just go nice and slowly

Okay now, hold your horses! This is a very significant piece of evidence. The royalists expected a long siege and for this reason they had stocked food in the town to last the garrison about nine months. It was only eight years previously that the town had been besieged by the Irish rebels, under the command of Sir Phelim O'Neill. For five long months no supplies could get into Drogheda. Eventually, in desperation, the population was reduced to eating dogs, horses and rats. Now here in 1649 with another siege looming it made sense to have the inhabitants removed. There was no military sense in feeding a 3,000-strong population of hungry mouths when the military occupants also numbered approximately 3,000. Can you imagine the arguments there might have been over the food if all the inhabitants had stayed? I imagine it would have had to be rationed. Mind you, if you wanted to lose weight, I suppose the best thing was to stay. Bulimics and anorexics would probably have chosen to stay. Vegetarians, vegans, celiacs and those who were lactose intolerant probably bailed because there would have been more healthy options on the outside. Trannies could just fend for themselves.

Dean Nicholas Bernard, a vicar at St Peter's Church, recorded that his wife and children had been evacuated from the town prior to Cromwell's arrival. It's impossible to know how many of the inhabitants departed from the town, but one has to assume it was a significant enough percentage to make a difference to the supply of available food for the defending army.

Food would also have been an issue for the attacking army. After all, there were approximately 12,000 Cromwellian troops camped all around the south side of the town. That's a lot of hungry bellies. In essence, the defenders held the advantage here as they had plenty of supplies. However, that depended on how long the siege was going to last. Cromwell had issued an appeal to country people throughout Ireland to come to his army and receive a fair price for their food. For too long now, marauding armies all over the country had stolen cattle, sheep and crops of all sorts with impunity to keep themselves alive. Money was always an issue for Cromwell in Ireland, but he still managed to feed his armies during his nine months there and his policy of paying the local farmers clearly paid off.

The plot Lady Wilmot had in the melting pot, and she gave it her best shot

Meanwhile, in the town before the mayhem ensued there was that civilian conspiracy already alluded to – an attempt to allow

Cromwell's troops into the place – which was orchestrated by a Lady Wilmot. See – that's not a well-publicised fact either, is it? A civilian coup? Within the town? To let Cromwell in? Are you havin' a laugh?

The fact is that, in general, the evidence concerning inhabitants preceding the siege suggests that either they were absent from the town, or they took up arms against the attackers, or they were engaged in an attempt to turn the town over to Cromwell. This is what we know. What we don't know is that people simply stayed in their houses, only emerging when they absolutely had to, and that they somehow got caught in the crossfire as a result. This is merely speculation and has no solid evidential platform.

It is important to analyse the information that has come down to us about the civilian population of the town. Those who make assumptions about the garrison being at their military posts and the civilians being present in their houses throughout the town as the walls were breached may well be mistaken. Turns out, a lot of people are mistaken about this stuff. It doesn't make sense. Nor does the evidence support it. On 10 September Cromwell sent a summons to the royalist governor of the town, Sir Arthur Aston. Aston had been placed in his position just a few weeks earlier by Ormond and he had as much of an affinity with the Boyneside town itself as the vast majority of his defending troops – who had only just arrived there to defend the place – which must have been very little. Effectively, by refusing to answer Cromwell's summons, Aston told Cromwell to shove it sideways up his arse.

The storm after the calm

There are any amount of books written about the storming of Drogheda in 1649, so I'm not going to go into any great detail here. Suffice to say, Cromwell battered his way through the impenetrable walls that were clearly penetrable, and the defenders ran for their Jaysus lives. What happened next is that there was *definitely* a massacre. Having researched the issue for some years now, I'm happy to say that this fact is completely incontrovertible. My only point in this whole sad affair is that it was confined to the military defenders, and that's the reason for this book. Just in case you missed that. No biggie. Just that. Cromwell gave the orders that nobody in arms was to be spared. He wanted to make a statement to the rest of the royalists in Ireland. And that statement was that if you mess with me, this is what will happen. So, he killed all the defenders. Well, anyone that wasn't savvy enough to get away. Turns out, there were plenty who escaped. This was the shock and awe of Drogheda. This was the massacre of the military defenders that would eventually become the myth of the massacre of the innocents.

Chaps be divils

In a political landscape such as this where fathers fought against sons, brothers against brothers, lovers against lovers, wives against husbands, it is difficult to conclude that the entire population of Drogheda were either fully on one side or the other – royalist or parliamentarian. Divisions were the order of the day, and those local royalist sympathisers who lived in Drogheda, and had the inclination, clearly took up arms to support the young sex-mad Prince Charles. (There isn't a lot of evidence to tell us that he was banging half of Paris, where he was in exile, but later in life he knocked seven bells outta many a buxom wench, the most famous of whom was seventeenth-century Hollywood starlet Nell Gwyn, every second Tuesday.) One of the defenders of Drogheda was the English royalist Edmund Verney, whose family had been ripped apart by the Civil War. He was a royalist, his father a parliamentarian. Verney, the poor bastard, was to die at Drogheda.

Sieges were quite the challenge for Cromwell. He hated them. He was much better as a cavalry commander in the field, where he had a proven record of success. This was where his experience was.

It all kicks off

At 5pm on Tuesday, 11 September 1649, from his tent that was pitched on an area now known as the Mount at Drogheda, Cromwell gave orders to Colonel James Castle to storm the walls of the town with his troops. The point was well chosen. Cromwell did not want to break up his army by sending any parties of men across the river to the northern side of the town. Castle's attempt to gain the breach ended in disaster. Castle himself was killed and his regiment were repulsed. Another attempt was made, and that too was repulsed by the defenders. But Cromwell himself decided that he would lead the third assault and that was the one that carried the day.

The evidence shows that as soon as the defenders realised the breach was lost, they retreated. All coordinated resistance seems to have ceased at this point. So not only did the New Model Army secure the churchyard, they also secured the entire town in one fell swoop, as many of the defenders simply ran away. This is an interesting point because while we don't have any definitive numbers, Lord Inchiquin, a former parliamentarian and the then royalist commander, received 'many' of the escapees at Trim, where he was ensconced:

Many men and some officers have made their escape out of Drogheda, amongst them Garret Dungan is one and is now at Tecraghan and Lieutenant-Colonel Cavanagh. Some of every regiment are come unto me. All conclude that No quarter was given there with Cromwell's leave but many were privately saved by officers and soldiers; the governor was killed after quarter was given by the officer that first came there, that some of the towers were defended until yesterday, quarter being denied them, and that yesterday morning the towers within they were blown up. That Varney, Finglass, Warren and some other officers were alive in the hands of some of Cromwell's officers twenty-four hours after the business was done, but whether their lives were obtained at Cromwell's hands or that they are yet living, they cannot tell.

When it comes to a discussion surrounding the different cohorts, for instance, there is never an estimated number given for those defenders who escaped from Drogheda. And yet, 'many' clearly did escape. This is the exact word that Inchiquin uses. Plenty of speculation, however, exists when it comes to the phrase 'many inhabitants'. The comparison itself is intrinsically interesting, is it not?

For Jaysus' sake, Micheál

Prof. Micheál Ó Siochrú, for one, has suggested that in the heat of the battle it was virtually impossible to distinguish between combatants and non-combatants and that's why civilians died. Let's just deal with this for a second, shall we?

Hardly an original idea (if you were paying attention earlier you should see what I did there), firstly, the clearest sign that an individual was an unarmed civilian was that he was *unarmed*. Babies and toddlers tended to be mostly unarmed in seventeenth-century sieges. Old women and children of all ages the same. It would be great if you'd distinguish between women and children and grown adult men in your published writings for once, professor. If civilians took up arms, then they were clearly in the posture of soldiers and could only expect to die, as Cromwell had forbidden his men to allow anyone found in arms to live. Such combatants would have had bandoliers, swords, muskets or pikes. The kind of stuff your average Joe would not have been wearing whilst popping out to the shops in the middle of a massacre.

We know many local men took up arms, because I have personally discovered that this was the case. Feck I'm good. Aren't I good? Worra bloke. So let's just consider the logistics for a second, shall we. You're a local who has taken up arms. The New Model Army – who all wore red coats – were massacring royalist soldiers on every street corner like it was going out of fashion. (We know they wore red coats. On 16 October 1649 an agreement between the Council of State and Richard Downes for supplying 16,000 coats and breeches for soldiers in Ireland stated:

> The coats to be made of Coventry or Gloucester cloth of Venice colour, red shrunk in cold water, all three-quarters and a nail in length, with tape strings, and bound about with the same...The breeches to be made of grey or other good colours, of Reading or other good cloth, 12,000 to be three-quarters and a half in length, and 4,000 three-quarters and a nail, well lined, and with hooks and buttons.

I'd like to thank Paul T. Wright for this information. But feck it, I won't.)

This was not a battle. It was a slaughter. It's not like you're going to miss this if you're on the streets of Drogheda at that time. Completely overwhelmed by superior numbers, you shit yourself. So, you sneak into a back alley and quickly discard your arms. Then you either make your way home or you shoot out the gate and head to Aunty Mary's house, which is miles away. We know that royalists in the English Civil War did not ever decide on a particular colour for a uniform.

Cromwell's soldiers were under strict instructions 'not to do any harm or violence to any persons whatsoever, unless they be in arms, or office with the enemy'. These were not unambiguous orders. They came from a commander who allegedly had two of his men hanged for stealing hens from an old woman on the way to Drogheda; a clear breach of this command. The New Model Army were no bunch of yokels with an arbitrary bloodlust for killing. This was a well-oiled, complex and sophisticated logistical military machine under strict orders. If you ditched your arms and there was no evidence that you had ever held any, you were exempt from the massacre. End of.

So, all things considered, Cromwell's men did not have any motivation to kill unarmed civilians. Period. Unfortunately, the good professor, from what I have seen and read, has never made the distinction between those grannies, grandads, uncles, mams, dads, toddlers and babies and what might have been a typical grown-up innocent man, who *might* in some weird bizarre parallel universe where the attackers were on drugs have been mistaken for a soldier. When you take into account the context of the civilians of Drogheda and their utter Englishness, his argument of arbitrary slaughter of the inhabitants of a typical Irish town or such like, and it didn't really matter who died, is completely demolished. From what I have seen, he never makes any attempt to quash the civilian atrocity stories, and his language has never allowed for women and children at worst – whatever about unarmed men – to have been completely exempt. Personally, I find this extremely objectionable.

That old 'and many inhabitants' chestnut again

According to Ormond, as we have seen, many local inhabitants who were anti-parliament also joined the defence of the town. This is also a significant point. Later, when the words 'and many inhabitants' would appear at the foot of a printed list of those 'slain at Drogheda', many historians would point to the three words as evidence of a civilian massacre. As we have already seen, this list would be printed in the official parliament pamphlet that also carried Cromwell's letter to the Speaker of the House, William Lenthall. Throughout the centuries it has been understood to be part of the letter that immediately precedes it in the pamphlet, and therefore has often been interpreted as Cromwell's own words.

However, as I discovered myself, on my lonesome, the list with the words actually first appeared in print five days before Cromwell even wrote his letter. Clearly this is not evidence of a civilian massacre, because as we now know from Ormond, many inhabitants were actually in arms. Ormond's words confirming that many inhabitants were armed have not been highlighted on a widespread basis in history books in the past.

Carnage and Skulduggery – the names of my next two goldfish

Those who did not flee from the town were mostly cut down in cold blood. Cromwell had forbidden his men to show mercy to anyone who was in arms. So, the scenes on the streets must have been horrific. Especially since the New Model army are only recorded as losing about a hundred men in all at Drogheda. That compares to approximately 3,000 royalist defenders. It must have been absolute carnage. A slaughter of epic proportions. Men must have been disarmed and then slain. Otherwise, the casualty total of the attackers would surely have been much higher, and the discrepancy proportionate. According to Cromwell, Ormond placed the 'flower of the Irish army' as defenders of Drogheda. So it's not like they were inexperienced rookies.

The accounts that have survived that discuss the events at Millmount imply that some skulduggery took place there. Arthur Aston and some of his men refused to give up Millmount until there was an agreement made that they would be spared their lives. However, as soon as they handed over their weapons, they were all cut down where they stood, including Aston, who was apparently killed with his own wooden leg. There is ambiguity as to whether or not Cromwell himself was directly responsible for this treachery. His subordinate Colonel Axtell was clearly involved.

Cromwell himself tells us that several of the defending soldiers climbed up into the steeple of St Peter's Church thinking that they might be safe. But it was Cromwell himself who gave the order for the pews in the church to be gathered under the steeple and set alight so that these 'barbarous wretches' would not escape his wrath. Men and bells came tumbling down in the ensuing inferno.

Take me to church

The rector of St Peter's Church in 1649 is a very interesting character. He was a vociferous opponent of both parliament and Cromwell, and the New Model Army knew his reputation. He had preached against parliament on many occasions and was a firm supporter of the monarchy. The Protestant Dean Nicholas Bernard wrote an account of the 1641 and 1649 sieges of Drogheda and is generally known as a reliable witness. An incident occurred at his own house that is interesting to note. Because of his reputation as a government agitator, a delegation arrived at his house to arrest him. There was some confusion at the front door and Bernard refused to come out. So, the Cromwellian soldiers fired through the door and a royalist quartermaster who was behind the door was hit, while his servant was killed. This incident has often been used to extrapolate the numbers of dead civilians as it was a domestic context (Bernard's residence) and a (potential) civilian was killed. One presumes that the civilian who died was 'in office' with the enemy, if he was the quartermaster's servant. In fact, he may even have been a member of the soldiery.

Other defenders occupied one or two of the towers that were set into the medieval curtain wall. From their lofty heights they used the windows and the safety of the top of the tower to snipe at the attackers. That took some balls under the circumcisions. There were discussions between these defenders and the attackers, and eventually the defenders capitulated and surrendered. However, on this occasion most of them were spared their lives. Only the officers and every tenth man were killed. The rest were shipped to Barbados where they would set up a rake of Irish bars. Interestingly, these were men who could have been killed according to the rules of war, but they were spared.

Pissing off Cromwell – you don't wanna do that

Following Drogheda, you will no doubt have noted that Cromwell proceeded to Wexford, where another massacre of soldiers took place. As we've already seen, this time about 1,500 defenders lost their lives. Between various sieges of towns, and places like Cork and other smaller Munster enclaves welcoming the parliamentarian army, by Christmas, Ireland was well on the way to being overwhelmed by an English army for the first time in its history.

During the winter break, in an attempt to galvanise resistance, the Catholic clergy met at Clonmacnoise. From this gathering, the prelates issued a call to arms in the form of a pamphlet that was to be printed and distributed countrywide in two instalments. In the text they stated that Cromwell's mission in Ireland was to 'extirpate' (destroy completely) the Catholic religion.

They further wrote that in order to extirpate the Catholic faith he would have to massacre, destroy or banish the entire Catholic population. When Cromwell got hold of this pamphlet at his winter quarters at Youghal in January, he became totally freaked out by it. He immediately sat down and penned a robust rejoinder. He was determined to get his point across. He insisted that it was the Catholic clergy who had destroyed the perfect peace that had existed in Ireland, since they had instigated the 1641 Rebellion. Parliament dreaded the very notion of Roman Catholicism and the prospect of such a despotic regime again finding a significant foothold in England. To them, this was a political entity that duped people into joining them, whose motives were more avaricious than spiritual.

These factors were uppermost in Cromwell's mind when he drafted his response to the prelates. It is interesting to note that the Catholic prelates made no mention whatsoever of civilian deaths at either Drogheda and Wexford in their call to arms. One would have thought that this was their opportunity to trigger the consciences of those whom they were trying to motivate. What better incentive for revenge could there possibly be than atrocities concerning women and children?

Cromwell's response to the prelates completely sums up his Irish campaign. Interestingly, out of 40 odd documents this is the only document that he wrote throughout his time in Ireland that contains the word 'catholic'. It was the Catholic clergy who were the source of Ireland's woes and it was they with whom he had major issues, not the people of Ireland. In this declaration alone, no fewer than *ten* times does he emphasise that unarmed folk were not to be harmed or suffer in any way at the hands of parliament; indeed on one occasion he explicitly denies that he had deliberately harmed any unarmed civilians whatsoever up to that point.

He even refers to the Catholic Church's deplorable past when telling them what he perceives to be God's directives: they should avoid the spirit of Cain, Corah and Balaam (whoever the feck they were – the three wise men, maybe?) by building the faith, not by forcing it on others, by praying to the Holy Ghost, not mumbling over matins, and most tellingly of all, 'not destroying men because they will not be of our Faith'. These do not seem like the words of a mass murderer. He is consistent in his compassionate approach to the ordinary Irish people from the moment he lands in Ireland. How many times do I gotta say this?!

Oh no, I didn't!

We have already seen that in the declaration Cromwell writes: 'But well, your words are, massacre, destroy and banish. Good now, give us an instance of one man since my coming into Ireland, not in arms, massacred, destroyed or banished, concerning the two first of which justice hath not been done, or endeavoured to be done.' He was keen from the start to quash any potential allegations of his inclusion of innocent civilians in a military conflict.

Sit back and relax

Okay, we need to take a break. This is the point in the story where you really need to pay attention. If you've been speed-reading up to now, this is the time to stop that shite. In order to get the gravitas of what I'm trying to say here, we need to slow the pace down. Got it? Okay, well, I'll start with a new paragraph.

Now, remember, I'm taking you through the events chronologically, as they happened. So back to your imagining process. Imagine for a second that it's still September 1649. And you're in Ireland. A massacre has taken place at Drogheda. This is big front-page news. Sharon Ní Bheoláin would be all over it on RTE. They would get days out of this. Weeks! People all over the place would know somebody who was in Drogheda. Eyewitnesses would be interviewed. The Internet would be broken. Escapees would tell horrific stories of a bloodbath. As news goes, even in the seventeenth century this was big. In the pubs and clubs all around the country people would be talking about very little else.

And just for the object of this particular exercise – let's say that Dan Sheedy's words (*History in Focus*, published by CJ

Fallon) that '3,500 inhabitants' of Drogheda were killed are accurate. Just for pig. The fact that the population was only estimated at 3,000 is purely academic at this stage. Let's keep with the 3,500. After all, that's what our kids are being taught here in 2023.

Not one of the people who were in Drogheda that day provides details of civilian deaths. If you look to the top of the page, you'll see that the title of this book is still *Making a Massacre*. In the days following the events, not a word has come down to us about a slaughter of innocents. So far, nobody thought of making that massacre of defenders into a civilian one.

Crouchy

However, beyant in England significant skulduggery was afoot. We've already discussed aspects of *The Man in the Moon*. Here's a few more that you can put in your pipe and smoke. One of Peter Crouch's ancestors, John Crouch, was just after hearing the news about Drogheda. John was what we would today call a conspiracy theorist. He was completely anti-government. Furthermore, he owned a newspaper he liked to call *The Man in the Moon*. John thought the name was hilarious but feck all of his readers got the in joke. In the last few years John had been in his element. This civil war had given him plenty to write about in his radical newspaper. John didn't really give a monkey's about publishing the truth. If his mouthpiece could help topple this bastard parliamentarian government then he was happy to help and he would publish outlandish lies at the drop of a hat. It was October 1649. John had just heard about the massacre of the royalist army at Drogheda.

Referring to the parliamentarian army, Crouch's *The Man in the Moon* (17–24 October 1649) states:

Their barbarous cruelty in that abhorrid act, not to be paralleled by any of the former massacres of the Irish, sparing neither women nor children, but putting them all to the sword. 3,000 indeed they killed, but 2,000 were women and children and divers aged persons that were not able to support themselves, much less able to resist them, the towne thus gained with the loss of 5,000 of their own.

Eager to paint the rebel parliamentarian army in as bad a light as possible, Crouchy claims that the parliamentarian army lost 5,000 men at Drogheda. This is a big miss. The losses on parliament's side at Drogheda are known to have been minuscule in comparison to the royalist casualties, 64 at the lowest estimate and 150 at the highest. McElligott even gives us more reason to doubt the veracity of *The Man in the Moon*. The following is an extract from a biography of John Crouch written by McElligott:

Crouch, John (b, c.1615, d in or after 1680), writer and bookseller, was born the son of a yeoman named Thomas Crouch in Standon, Hertfordshire. He had at least one brother, Gilbert Crouch, who acted as a land agent for the earl of Shrewsbury. John Crouch began an apprenticeship with the bookseller Nicholas Salisbury on 6 November 1632 and served his time until 2 December 1639. He evidently worked as a bookseller during the 1640s and there is no evidence that he wrote any books or pamphlets during the 1630s. Between 1652 and 1657 he and a printer named Thomas Wilson owned and ran a print shop at the sign of the Three Foxes in Long Lane in Smithfield. In February 1648 Crouch wrote the first part of a two-part satirical, anti-puritan pamphlet entitled *Craftie Cromwell*. Between April and November 1648 he wrote five further anti-puritan pamphlets, the Kentish Fayre, and four plays based on the character of Mrs Parliament. He also wrote three numbers of a royalist newsbook entitled *Mercurius Critticus* and a counterfeit edition of John Hackluyt's royalist newsbook *Mercurius Melancholicus*. In April 1649 he wrote the first of fifty-seven issues of *The Man in the Moon*. The eight-page weekly was printed by John's kinsman Edward Crouch. It recounted little news and relied instead on obscene stories and rhymes to fill its pages. Its principal targets were parliament, the army, the council of state and the official newsbooks. In general it had three main lines of attack: the humble social origins of England's new rulers, their alleged sexual immorality, and their contempt for, and oppression of, the poor.

Georgie

George Wharton (1617–1681) was an astrologer and royalist who published annual polemical almanacs during the mid-seventeenth century that drew him into fierce battles in print with his parliamentarian rivals. In 1645 he was commissioned captain of a regiment of horse, and fought for the king for a couple of years, after which he returned to writing. In his *Bellum Hybernicale* (December 1646) he antagonised parliament further when he justified the rebellion of 1641 in Ireland on the grounds of Ireland's long history of repression and suggested that the English and Scots were equally to blame for the massacres. (Steady on there, Georgie...) He was horrified when the king was executed, and in his almanac of 1650 he described parliament as 'the most prodigious Monsters that ever the earth groaned under' and he threatened them with execution and hell-fire themselves, an act for which he was subsequently arrested. Quite the dreamboat was Mr Wharton. A great catch.

Wharton's *Mercurius Elencticus,* dated 15 October 1649, says that the New Model Army 'possessed themselves of the towne and used all cruelties imaginable on the besieged, as well inhabitants and others, sparing neither women nor children'.

Of Wharton and other royalist newsbook writers, historian Jason McElligott has written:

All of these men penned propaganda in a variety of formats during their time at Oxford, and they probably knew each other well. It has been noted above that a pamphlet written in 1644 suggested that Birkenhead, Taylor and Wharton met once a week in a tavern in Oxford to muster up whole regiments of lies, slanders and ridiculous quibbles against the Parliament and the city of London.

In short, Wharton was a propagandist who simply printed what he wanted to print. The way newspapers worked in those days was that if you had an opinion, the requisite funds and access to a printing press, you could print whatever the hell you liked and disseminate it among the multitudes with gay abandon. There were licensing laws that pertained to printers, but circumventing the law was easy when the laws were made by parliament, and royalists clearly had differing views on what news should be promulgated.

As I said, it is a piece of piss to dismiss the allegations of Wharton and Crouch out of hand. Firstly, they were clearly extreme polemicists, who were not in Drogheda when the events occurred, had axes to grind, and would stop at nothing to spread lies and calumny about their enemies in a time of war. So, while on the face of it some historians continue to use these accounts as evidence of a civilian massacre, it is clear that an objective analysis of this 'evidence' will render it totally impotent. How in the Jame of Naysus can you take *anything* they say seriously?!

In the chronology of the events, it would seem prudent to evaluate the primary source evidence: the contemporary documents that were written at the exact time. Society was quite sophisticated, and as we've seen already the literacy rate was around 30 to 40 per cent. So, if thousands or even hundreds of innocent people were massacred at Drogheda, how likely is it that we would be depending on the disinformation of two royalist hacks to substantiate these stories? Surely someone, somewhere, would have written something about it? This is a classic case of the fact that a lie can be halfway around the world before the truth even has its shoes on.

Then there's those local records – remember them?

This is the shit that got me excited when I was pretending to be a historian all those years ago. The actual words of the people of Drogheda, who are speaking to us across the centuries. At a Corporation meeting on 7 October 1658 (a month after Cromwell's death), there is an entry that suggests that the municipal authorities were well out of harm's way at the time of the storm. Jonas Ellwood, who was an alderman and perhaps a brother of the mayor in September 1649, William Ellwood, was granted a lease of 'the lower seller under the Tholsell: for sixty and one yeares at the rent of twenty shillings per Ann. Provided that in case of Warrs or Rebellion the Corporacon if required may make use thereof for that present occasion.' It may be surmised that like all of the townspeople, they knew only too well to be either out of town or off the streets during the time of an assault on the town. Naturally, as the town fathers, they had their choice of secure hideaways.

When the Corporation reconvened at Michaelmas 1649, all of its members were in a state of perfect health. It is obvious from the handwriting that the minutes of the April Assembly were written in October after Cromwell had left. At the General Assembly of 5 October (the venue is not given), the names are the same as those who attended the April meeting, which took place at the Tholsel. Contained in the Corporation minute book are the names of hundreds of civilians who went about their normal daily business in the days, weeks and months following the storm. It is useless to suggest that these were new English planters because the timeframe makes it impossible, and in any case, no proof exists to substantiate it.

If the whole community had been obliterated in mid-September, how likely is it that it would be completely replenished by 5 October with the full mechanism of local government completely restored?! Only three days earlier, Samuel Porter had arrived in London carrying the packages containing Cromwell's letters to the ruling body in London, announcing the official news that Drogheda had fallen. At that time in Drogheda, life was as normal as it could have been under the circumstances. Free members were admitted to the Corporation, leases were granted, gate customs were collected, and petitions were granted and refused. The entire population killed, my feckin' ass.

Okay, so we have now established that there is no factual basis to the civilian massacre story on any scale in the primary source documents. Now, I'm no historian (have I mentioned this already?) but I'm just trying to work out when the sources cease to become 'primary source'. Wharton and Crouch wrote their shite in October 1649, just weeks after the events, so they can probably be considered 'primary source' – although in a way I would also contest that. They weren't there. They didn't witness a damn thing. But I have noticed that some historians call them primary sources. Now, you have the perfect right to disagree with me here and decide that you want to believe Wharton and Crouch. Go for it. For my part, I prefer to believe me. Sorry, I mean the facts.

The silence about Wexford is deafening

So, the biggest things to hit the headlines in Ireland in 1649 were Drogheda and of course Wexford. You might think that by November, a month after Wexford, Wharton and Crouch would make the same accusations about Cromwell's storming of the resort town of the sunny south-east. Well, you'd be wrong. They didn't. You might also think that some royalist propagandist somewhere in the world in 1649 would publish a story that states innocent civilians were slaughtered at Wexford. Well, you'd be wrong here too. Because that simply didn't happen. Now, isn't that odd?

The year 1649 closed and no letter, newspaper or pamphlet, private letter or declaration of any sort was printed anywhere to indicate that innocent civilians were massacred at either Drogheda or Wexford. Even as the year turned and the country rang in the New Year of 1650, you might well think that somebody somewhere would say it, because technically, I'm guessing, we're still in the 'primary source' realm, although it must be starting to wane.

After Cromwell left Ireland in May 1650, nothing was said about civilian fatalities. Both licensed and unlicensed pamphlets and newsbooks were produced in their thousands and still nothing during the next few years. In fact, we should probably do this in a tabulated format, just to emphasise the passing of the years.

Year	Civilian atrocity reports
1649	Wharton & Crouch
1650	Nada
1651	Zilch
1652	Zero
1653	Naught
1654	Zip

1655	Didley-squat
1656	Nil
1657	Nowt
1658	None
1659	Jackshit
1660	The Return of the King – all hell breaks loose

What's another year?

So, bear with me here – by 1653 Cromwell's meteoric rise through the military ranks in England saw him installed as Lord Protector. There were still plenty of detractors, particularly here in Ireland, as landowners lost their lands in a dramatic alteration in the landscape of property ownership. Yet there was nothing that spoke of large numbers of the inhabitants of Drogheda being killed, or how that would affect the local economy and the general conditions of the town. The Corporation records do not tell that story. The years passed.

The 1650s carried on and still nothing was said regarding civilian deaths at Drogheda or Wexford. So, let's just follow the chronological order of this whole civilian massacre thing and see where it gets us. And remember – so far all we have are Wharton & Crouch.

By the year 1658, Cromwell's detractors far outnumbered his supporters. Like any head of government, I suppose. But of course here we had the regicide undercurrent, which gave his critics significant motivation. When he died, there was a flurry of commendatory narratives published, as one might expect.

After Cromwell's death in 1658, his son Richard assumed the role of Lord Protector. But as we already noted, Richard was a feckin' disaster. He was placed under house arrest in 1659 and the army did a deal with the young bodice-ripper Prince Charles, who was restored to the throne on 29 May 1660, his thirtieth birthday, horny as a rabbit in heat.

And so, it begins

This is another key to this story. Now the political environment was changed drastically. Now the making of the massacre begins in earnest. Charles II went on a revenge mission and sought out all the regicides who had signed his father's death warrant. Furthermore, he essentially decreed that Cromwell's republic had effectively never happened. Those who wanted to curry favour with the Stuart dynasty couldn't get to the printing presses quickly enough to print all sorts of lies and calumny against the recent republic. It was at this stage that the stories began to emerge of wholesale civilian fatalities in Ireland. Although Charles was happy to retain the legacy of the 'Cromwellian' settlement of Ireland, the bulk of the other policies of the Interregnum were cast aside.

In his book *God's Executioner*, Micheál Ó Siochrú writes: 'By the 1660s, following the restoration of Charles II, Irish clerical sources confidently asserted that 4,000 civilians had died in Drogheda, the result of "an unparalleled savagery and treachery beyond that of any slaughterhouse".'

Good man, Micheál! And they accused *me* of abusing Irish history?! Seriously? Why would you even do that? *Are you seriously asking people to believe that the Irish Catholic prelates completely forgot that 4,000 civilians had died when they wrote their original two declarations in the winter of 1649 following Drogheda and Wexford?* The same declaration that was designed to galvanise royalist opposition to Cromwell throughout the country? Didn't you even think for a second that the post-1660 sources you used were using any means available to them to join in the Cromwell bashing? There weren't even 4,000 civilians living in Drogheda at the time! And now everybody who was killed was a civilian?! Grrr. Wash your keyboard out with soap. It's a travesty that this stuff is still being taught to students of history in Irish universities today.

The post-Restoration Wexfordian chancers

Twelve years after the events at Wexford, on 21 May 1661, the petition of the people of Wexford to Charles II was read out in parliament. This document has made a considerable impact on our interpretation of what exactly happened at both Drogheda and Wexford.

In the early twentieth century (1905), historian Robert Pentland Mahaffy published the *Calendar of State Papers Relating to Ireland, 1660–1662* in which he reproduces (most of) the actual petition on page 336. However, concerning the sentence that relates the number of dead, Mahaffy prints the following sentence: 'The governor and 1,500 men lost their lives, and the property of the inhabitants became pillage to the usurper's soldiers.' Mahaffy worked on the State Papers for 18 years, from 1896 to 1914. On the face of it, his assiduous transcription of the State Papers does not facilitate bias, so it is interesting to note that while paraphrasing the petition, his interpretation of the petition is that 1,500 was the total killed, and that they were all 'men'.

This document is still in existence, and it is these words that are the most incriminating to Cromwell. Bizarre as it may seem, they could be seen to totally impeach *every single* eyewitness account, even those that were written by the hands of the Confederate defenders themselves. Any study of the storming of Wexford is compounded by the expressions contained in this controversial document. This was a climate when the beleaguered population of Ireland optimistically flooded the new monarch with petitions in order to erase the memory of the devastating Cromwellian period from the country at large. The Wexford document was composed immediately after the Restoration in an effort by some locals to obtain restitution of their properties and possessions. The first reference on it is dated 4 July, and the next, a certificate, dated 21 May 1661.

It probably took a year to reach the king himself. There is no recorded reply. It was generally the case with most comparable appeals of the time that they were totally ignored by a king who had neither the authority nor the desire to get involved in such trivialities.

They opened the petition with confirmation of their loyalty to England by reminding the king that they had promised to make ten ships for the royal cause early in the war, and they also declared that they 'have always been a people adhering to the interest of the Crowne and ancient Collonies since the reigne of King Henry the second'. After declaring that upon Cromwell's arrival before the town, they had been ready to 'expose their lives and fortunes for the defence' of their town, they continued to implore Charles II for atonement, by announcing that they 'doe most humbly beseech your Majestie to be graciously pleased to look on them as deserved objects of your favour and justice'.

However you dress it up, it just dozen ring true

No bother to me to refute the statements contained in this document, however audacious if not downright foolhardy this might seem. It has always been described as having been written by the surviving friends and relations of the dead innocent civilians. It might appear that this document alone confirms the deaths of innocents at both Drogheda and Wexford, and for some people, there the story should end. Even the most objective of historians have treated its content with respect. The problem is that it just *does not work*.

It simply does not fit into the primary source accounts of the storming of that town 11 years earlier. If taken in the context of the period following the collapse of the parliamentary revolution that saw the accession of Charles II to the throne (with reduced powers), the essence of the affidavit arouses suspicion. The use of the term 'Usurper' that it contains confirms the regard with which Cromwell was then held. This term was widely in use in post-Restoration England and including it in any document immediately exposed the writer's royalist sympathies. Now that he was dead and the primary target of Restoration contempt, these casualties of war would take every opportunity to further blacken his name. Firstly, the petitioners give a figure of 1,500 dead, which (similar to Drogheda) is precisely the official number of fallen armed defenders. There is absolutely no room in the figures to account for every 'man, woman and child to a very few' having being killed. It can be further discredited by the manner in which it describes the sacking of Drogheda as an indiscriminate slaughter and says that *all* of the inhabitants were killed there. My effen bollix.

The smears of James Heath

In 1663, 14 years after the events, the royalist James Heath, who had no credentials to be an authority on the Irish campaign, wrote a scurrilous biography of Cromwell and 'confidently asserted' that 300 women were killed around the market cross in Wexford. More bullshit. Oddly, Heath says nothing whatsoever of civilian deaths at Drogheda. In fairness, he was only making stuff up, so his imagination just didn't go there.

Much later allegations from the pens of spurious others

Historical sources are mad yokes. The further away from 1649 they become, the less relevant they are. Other accounts – like the well-known sources Dr George Bate, Edward Hyde, the Earl of Clarendon, the memoirs of Bullstrode Whitelocke, and Edmund Ludlow – all say shit about Cromwell massacring civilians but obviously add nothing to the debate as none were eyewitnesses and all wrote their missives with prejudice tens of years later.

So now we are about to leave the seventeenth century and what do we have so far to convict Cromwell of a massacre of unarmed civilians in Ireland? Jack effen shit, that's what! Unless of course, you're a mad nationalist and you're buying none of this. BTW this is not a subheading. I just writ it this large to emphasise the point.

The eighteenth century and beyond

During the eighteenth century, Cromwell largely faded into obscurity. This was mainly because he was dead. At the start of that century the writer Isaac Kimber, in his biography *The Life of Oliver Cromwell: Lord Protector of the Commonwealth of England, Scotland, and Ireland. Impartially collected from the best historians, and several original manuscripts*, blamed Cromwell's son in-law and the Levellers (their participation in all of this is not for the likes of this book) for the execution of the king, and he rationalised the events at Drogheda, saying that they saved bloodshed in the long run.

The Earl of Clarendon's history of the wars emerged in 1702, and he just went off on one. Regarding Drogheda, he wrote that fear so possessed the defenders

> that they threw down their arms upon a general offer of quarter; so that the enemy entered the works without resistance, and put every man, governor, officer, and soldier, to the sword; and the whole army being entered the town, they executed all manner of cruelty, and put every man that related to the garrison, and all the citizens who were Irish, man, woman, and child, to the sword.

Ah yeah, the guy just added fuel to the massacre flames and wrote what he wanted to write, whether he actually believed it or not. For some odd reason, Clarendon's words became important for others who came after him with an agenda.

Otherwise, as all the Georges (the first, second and third) got on with ruling England during this century, Cromwell was mostly cast to the mists of time. And sure, why would he not be?

Carlyle's Cromwell versus Murphy's Cromwell

Then in 1845 the Scottish historian and writer Thomas Carlyle – whom we have already met – dedicated much of his spare time to writing volumes of stuff about his hero Oliver Cromwell. His work made a seismic impact on Cromwell's story. Carlyle hailed Cromwell as a total hero. In his *Letters and Speeches of Oliver Cromwell*, for the first time ever, people could actually read the words of the man himself.

Turned out he wasn't such a bollix.

The actual making of the massacre

Much later, at the end of the nineteenth century, the abundant anti-British sentiment pouring from the pens of Irish nationalists helped to further endorse seventeenth-century propaganda, and as a result, embed the facts in an indecipherable historical morass. When the revamped and triumphalist Catholic Church took centre stage in Irish life at this time, one of its first manifestations was a thorough revision of Irish history to emphasise the indestructible age-old bond between Catholicism and the Irish nation. In this narrative Cromwell was a vital character. As we've already seen, new books like Murphy's *Cromwell in Ireland* (1883) created a politically correct Catholic version of Cromwell, one that was accepted universally and without reservation.

Since then, Murphy's analysis has largely stood firm as an accurate version of events. Also, a major contributor to the massacre story was John P. Prendergast's *The Cromwellian Settlement of Ireland*, which was published in 1868. Both

Prendergast and Murphy wanted to make Cromwell look as bad as possible and so they made use of the Wood tract and the hyperbole of the Irish Catholic clergy, who just invented stuff years after the events and castigated Cromwell from a veritable height.

People dug into the vast reservoir of old news-sheets and began to use the disinformation of Wharton and Crouch to support their civilian massacre allegations. And of course, sure didn't Cromwell himself say that he killed 'many inhabitants'? It was all feckin' gris to the 'making a massacre' mill.

And would you look at the petition of the people of Wexford – how could you argue with that? There was any amount of seventeenth-century propaganda that Irish writers, who were promised they were going to be 'A Nation Once Again', could now find to construct the 'we hate the Brits' narrative, and they did just that. In their droves.

Would yis ever foot the shuck up

It is the responsibility of the historians to stop using the word 'civilians' or 'townspeople' in the context of those who were slaughtered at Drogheda. The implication here is that they were ordinary, non-military people who were either deliberately or accidentally killed – as I said before, the mothers, the fathers, grannies, grandads, aunts, uncles, teenagers, children, toddlers. The evidence clearly suggests that the extraordinary severity that was used by Cromwell at Drogheda was confined to the military defenders. It is my opinion that the population was all but evacuated. There were fewer mouths to feed that way.

I'm not exactly sure what all of this says about my country. For anybody who is not Irish, I can tell you now that just simmering beneath the surface of most Irish people is a hatred of the English. It's impossible for ordinary folk here to separate the oppression that Ireland has suffered over the centuries from its larger neighbour, the bulldog bully. And so, we seem to want to hold that grudge about Cromwell. We almost need to have it to feed the victim narrative. Memories of the Famine, when England turned its face from Ireland and, some would say, contributed largely to the outrageous death toll with its abject indifference to our country's plight, are not that faded. They're merely a few generations old. It doesn't take much for Irish hearts to stir when it comes to our embattled past. As far as I'm concerned, I'm perfectly happy to have been oppressed by English oppression like any other Irish person and that feeling is just simmering below my skin as well. But I say we should pick our battles. And Cromwell is not one of them. It is Henry Ireton, Charles Fleetwood, Edmund Ludlow, and a plethora of other anonymous parliamentarian generals, officials and officers who we should blame for the atrocities of the mid-seventeenth century. Not Oliver Cromwell.

The weaponising of Irish history

In the North of Ireland of course there has always been an extra potency to Irish history, as it has consistently been used to embellish age-old animosities between loyalists and nationalists. Cromwell has been used to justify atrocities there during the Troubles. There are murals of him in full living colour on the gable ends of houses to interpret as you will, depending on your politics and cultural background. It doesn't take much for a nationalist to point to the fact that Cromwell was the one who was significantly responsible for the partition of the island, since it was effectively his military campaign that copper-fastened the English plantations. At the time of writing, there are noises being made about border polls taking place, and the possibility of a united Ireland is under discussion. If we can manage to extricate Cromwell from the serious charges of genocide, in my opinion we're facilitating those old nuggets of peace and reconciliation, and what possible harm is there in that? This is a 'good news' story. Okay, it's turning history on its head. But surely that's gotta be a good thing. I can't wait to tackle the Battle of the Boyne. Some people are gonna be pretty pissed when I discover that it was James who really won.

When, as a belligerent amateur, I began to openly question the work of the academics Ó Siochrú, Lenihan, McElligott and Morrill, to name but a few, they simply closed ranks. It is difficult to fully appreciate the reasons why this occurred. Historians are fallible too. Some often appear as gatekeepers to the facts. But discerning students of history will see that there is a clear lack of evidence to support the civilian massacre tradition at Drogheda. I am completely convinced that this miscarriage of historical justice will be ultimately redressed in the world. But maybe not in my lifetime.

In fairness, and generally speaking, my books on Cromwell (the modest numbers that have been sold to date) have been well received, and ordinary non-academicy people (but not nearly enough) are beginning to accept the clarity of the facts. It's becoming more and more difficult to dispute my arguments. So, the historians can keep their ranks closed. Shove your closed ranks up your asses, boys. As the years pass, the truth will emerge, despite the best efforts of some people to cherish and foster an age-old grudge that promotes anti-Englishness.

In the end, I suppose despite my vehement protestations over the years, I have become what they call an amateur historian. If the cap fits. I had been fighting any sort of a historian tag for a long time simply because of my Leaving Cert results and lack of third-level education and I was getting off on that fact. But now, in my twilight years, I have come to embrace it. In fact, I'm a bit of an auld trailblazer. And soon everyone will be following my trail.

Further exoneration – weed it and reap

Elsewhere, contemporary research is now proving that Cromwell's name is gradually being extricated from what is commonly known the 'Cromwellian Plantation'. The wonderful historian John Cunningham has shown that parliament's Irish government had to move to prevent Catholic Irish landowners from petitioning Cromwell as Lord Protector for restoration of their lands because he invariably displayed clemency in these cases. Cunningham says: 'Many of the agreements that Cromwell had made with the Irish were reneged on by others who came after him.' According to Cunningham:

> While the massacre at Drogheda in 1649 remains a blot on his reputation, in the 1650s Cromwell in fact emerged as an important and effective ally for Irish landowners seeking to defeat the punitive confiscation and transplantation policies approved by the Westminster parliament and favoured by the Dublin government. In his extensive dealings with Irish landowners, he displayed a genuine compassion for cases of hardship and a strong aversion to perceived unfairness and injustice. Moreover, it is clear that the Catholics and Protestants who made approaches to Cromwell fully expected to be treated equitably and honourably by him, and nothing that had occurred during the conquest of Ireland was sufficient to dampen their expectations.

But that's a kettle of a different colour of horses and we're definitely not getting into any more detail here. Suffice to say – don't believe everything you read. Except for this. You need to believe this!

You should always finish with a flourish, so here goes nothin'

The Drogheda churchyards of St Mary's and St Peter's Church of Ireland in my home town reek of history today. Stepping in from the street to either location, one is immediately enveloped by a sense of the past. The walls, the ground, the air, all speak of the horrendous massacre. The good, the bluts. It's about time we changed that legacy to reflect the facts. Only then can we begin to deal with the negative local tradition that residents of the town were the victims of English savagery that is engrained in Drogheda's identity.

As we've seen, the town's 828-year-old history is actually more allied to an English/Protestant legacy than an Irish/Catholic one. Cromwell's troops had neither orders nor motive to kill any innocents left in Drogheda or Wexford. Nor is there any solid evidence to suggest they did. With the revelations that I myself have recently made in the course of my research, it is only now that the full story can be accurately told.

I'm hoping I've made it pretty clear that I'm not the one who is abusing Irish history. If I haven't achieved this for *you* in particular, my dear reader, then you've clearly got issues. Or to put it another way – maybe you'll be the one to take me down. G'wan! Shut me up. But you'll have to explain yourself. Take your best shot. You won't win. I am utterly imperious. And my case in Cromwell's favour is sock rolid.

To finish this book it is probably best to simply repeat Cromwell's famous, poignant and oft-quoted words, 'It's pronounced Leedle, yis feckin' eejits, not Liddle!'

The past has ended. Go in peace.

Liberalis is a Latin word which evokes ideas of freedom, liberality, generosity of spirit, dignity, honour, books, the liberal arts education tradition and the work of the Greek grammarian and storyteller Antoninus Liberalis. We seek to combine all these inter-linked aspects in the books we publish.

We bring classical ways of thinking and learning in touch with traditional storytelling and the latest thinking in terms of educational research and pedagogy in an approach that combines the best of the old with the best of the new.

As classical education publishers, our books are designed to appeal to readers across the globe who are interested in expanding their minds in the quest of knowledge. We cater for primary, secondary and higher education markets, homeschoolers, parents and members of the general public who have a love of ongoing learning.

If you have a proposal that you think would be of interest to Liberalis, submit your inquiry in the first instance via the website: www.liberalisbooks.com.